Flipping Houses For Cash

How are so many people getting rich flipping houses and why aren't you?

A J Smith

© **Copyright 2019 - All rights reserved.**

The content contained within this book may not be reproduced, duplicated or transmitted without direct written permission from the author or the publisher.

Under no circumstances will any blame or legal responsibility be held against the publisher, or author, for any damages, reparation, or monetary loss due to the information contained within this book. Either directly or indirectly.

Legal Notice:

This book is copyright protected. This book is only for personal use. You cannot amend, distribute, sell, use, quote or paraphrase any part, or the content within this book, without the consent of the author or publisher.

Disclaimer Notice:

Please note the information contained within this document is for educational and entertainment purposes only. All effort has been executed to present accurate, up to date, and reliable, complete information. No warranties of any kind are declared or implied. Readers acknowledge that the author is not engaging in the rendering of legal, financial, medical or professional advice. The content within this book has been derived from various sources. Please consult a licensed professional before attempting any techniques outlined in this book.

By reading this document, the reader agrees that under no circumstances is the author responsible for any losses, direct or indirect, which are incurred as a result of the use of information contained within this document, including, but not limited to, — errors, omissions, or inaccuracies.

Table of Contents

INTRODUCTION	9
SECTION 1: A BRIEF HISTORY OF REAL ESTATE	10
CHAPTER 1: FROM OUR HOUSE TO YOURS	10
CHAPTER 2: WHY SO MUCH SUCCESS?	13
CHAPTER 3: HOW CAN YOU EARN 6 FIGURES THROUGH REAL ESTATE?	15
SECTION 2: MINDSET + LIES	19
CHAPTER 4: THE LIES OF THE 9-5	19
CHAPTER 5: THE LIE OF MONEY	21
CHAPTER 6: THE LIE OF GETTING RICH QUICK	23
CHAPTER 7: HOW TO GET AHEAD	27
CHAPTER 8: CREATURE OF HABIT	30
SECTION 3: INCREASE YOUR KNOWLEDGE	33
CHAPTER 9: LET'S START AT THE BEGINNING	33
CHAPTER 10: RISKS	39
CHAPTER 11: WHAT DO YOU WANT OUT OF LIFE?	42

CHAPTER 12: WHY YOU SHOULD DO IT ANYWAY   **45**

SECTION 4: THE SECRETS THEY DON'T WANT YOU TO KNOW   **48**

CHAPTER 13: SUMMARY OF THE REAL ESTATE INDUSTRY IN 2019   **48**

CHAPTER 14: SECRETS OF THE REAL ESTATE INDUSTRY   **51**

CHAPTER 15: THE MOST COMMON WAYS THE REAL ESTATE INDUSTRY TAKES ADVANTAGE OF YOU   **54**

CHAPTER 16: HOW TO BE TAKEN SERIOUSLY AS A FIRST-TIME BUYER   **57**

SECTION 5: FINDING THE RIGHT HOUSE   **64**

CHAPTER 18: COUNTING DOWN THE CLOCK   **69**

CHAPTER 19: WHERE TO LOOK TO FIND FLIPPABLE PROPERTIES   **71**

CHAPTER 20: APARTMENTS + HOUSES   **78**

CHAPTER 21: FORECLOSURES   **81**

CHAPTER 22: EXTERNAL FACTORS   **83**

CHAPTER 23: THE LAWS   **87**

SECTION 6: VIEWING AND BUYING   **91**

CHAPTER 24: THE CHECKLIST	91
CHAPTER 25: DO THE NUMBERS ADD UP?	95
CHAPTER 26: HOW TO GET CAPITAL	99
CHAPTER 27: CLOSING THE DEAL	103
SECTION 7: LET'S MAKE SOME MONEY	109
CHAPTER 28: INCREASING THE VALUE	109
CHAPTER 29: WHAT TO FIX?	112
CHAPTER 30: DIY VS. CONTRACTING	116
CHAPTER 31: NEGOTIATING WITH CONTRACTORS	120
CHAPTER 32: OUTSIDE REVAMP	123
SECTION 8: GET READY TO SELL	125
CHAPTER 33: HOW TO SELL	125
CHAPTER 34: NO ONE BUYING?	128
CHAPTER 35: CLOSE THE DEAL	130
CHAPTER 36: ONGOING MINDSET	133
CHAPTER 37: MISTAKE OF THE 99%	135
CHAPTER 38: FINAL CHECKLIST	139

CHAPTER 39: KEEPING THE PROPERTY FOR RENT 142

CONCLUSION 147

REFERENCES 148

Introduction

I want to thank you for choosing this book, and I hope you enjoy reading it.

Real estate has always been a lucrative investment option because of the potential it offers. There are different ways in which you can generate passive income from real estate investment. One of the most popular ways to attain financial independence is by flipping houses.

In this book, you will learn everything you need to know about real estate investing, especially about flipping houses in order to become a successful investor. This book will be your guide as you wade through the waters of real estate investing. Now, all that you need to do is take the first step and carefully go through the information given in this book. Once you understand what you need to do, you will be that much closer to achieving the financial freedom you always wanted.

So, why don't we get started?

Section 1: A Brief History of Real Estate

Chapter 1: From Our House to Yours

The real estate industry includes the development, management, marketing, leasing and selling of residential, commercial, industrial and agricultural properties. Any changes in the local and national economies influence the price movement in this industry. However, it is one of the most lucrative forms of investment because the need for space is steadily increasing while the space available is limited. The more limited a resource, the greater is its demand and value.

The history of real estate in the United States is quite long and diverse. The era of private ownership of land was ushered in after the Revolutionary War with the federal government selling and granting and land to private owners. This went on until the introduction of the Homestead Act in 1862, which provided for the private ownership of land in the U.S. for at least five years for the property's improvement and development. Under the Homestead Act, over 300 million acres of public property were handed over to private landowners, and this created the real estate market.

The evolution of the real estate industry progressed as the U.S. went from being an agrarian economy to an industrial one. Urban centers sprouted at the onset of the Industrial Revolution, and people shifted to cities to look for employment in factories. The workers not only needed a place to reside, but they needed to be able to afford it too. The progress of industrial, banking, and other financial sectors increased the U.S.A.'s wealth. This meant the middle class, as well as the blue-collar workers, were now able to gain mortgages, which in turn gave rise to home ownership.

Urbanization leads to an increase in real estate transactions. There was a sudden boom in the real estate industry with different offices, retail spaces, hotels, restaurants, and residential properties sprouting up everywhere. This led to the creation of the cities and towns we see today.

Even years after the inception of the real estate industry, it is still one of the most lucrative aspects of the U.S. economy as it not only is an income generating machine but also provides different career opportunities. There are various aspects involved in this industry. Brokers and agents assist in leasing and selling properties. Developers purchase the land, develop it, and then sell it to others. Building managers help property owners to manage their properties, whereas appraisers assess the value of properties before their sale. Apart from this, there are others involved like real estate lawyers, office managers, loan officers, and support staff who are a part of real estate transactions.

During the mid-2000s, the real estate industry faced a tough time after there was a significant boom in real estate, which was followed by a steep decline that led to a recession. However, the market has certainly strengthened since then, and it is steadily improving. In 2014, over $1.1 trillion was generated from real estate construction and accounted for over 6% of the nation's GDP. Regardless of how strong or weak an economy is, there will always be a need for spaces to live, work, and shop and this is the reason for the strong position the real estate industry holds.

Chapter 2: Why So Much Success?

Why are so many people interested in investing in the real estate market? Here are all the benefits real estate investment offers.

Good returns

The returns it offers are better than the ones generated by the stock market sans the volatility. The risk of loss in real estate is often reduced due to the duration for which you hold the property. As the market improves, the value of your property increases, and this, in turn, increases your equity. Real estate also offers a greater degree of control over your investment since the property you own is a tangible asset that can be readily used to capitalize on other revenue streams while benefiting from property appreciation.

Tangibility

Real estate always has tangible asset value since the value of land or property is something you will always have in hand. Other investments tend to leave you with little or even no tangible asset value, like stocks that can plummet to zero or an asset like a car whose value depreciates over time. Any insurance you have on real estate will help safeguard your property if a worst-case scenario comes true.

Appreciation

The value of the real estate increases with time. Historically speaking, the longer you hold onto the property, the higher the amount you stand to gain. The real estate market always recovers from the cycles of boom and recession. If you hold onto the property when the market is bleak, the property will appreciate once the market stabilizes.

Diversification

It helps diversify your investment portfolio. Diversification is essential for any investor since it helps spread out the risk of investment across different instruments. Having a relatively safe and tangible asset in your portfolio helps mitigate the risk of investment.

Tax benefits

Apart from all this, there are also various tax benefits and concessions you can claim by investing in real estate. The tax benefits offered on real estate are unlike any on other instruments of investment. If you have a mortgage on the property, you can deduct the mortgage interest along with any operating costs, insurance expenses, property taxes, and depreciation on the property. Saving on your tax payments helps increase your cash flow.

Chapter 3: How Can You Earn 6 Figures Through Real Estate?

Investing in real estate will help to increase your cash flow. If you become a good investor, you can start earning 6 figures through your investments. However, to do this, you must know the different aspects of investing in real estate, have a solid plan of action and do the necessary tasks to attain your financial independence. There are various things you must do to become a successful investor, and they are as follows.

Change Your Mindset About Investing

Success depends as much on your actions as it does on your mindset. Having a success mindset is essential to becoming a successful investor. In this section, you will learn about why a 9-5 job isn't all that it claims to be, the common misconceptions about money mindset and how to change your perception about money, the habits you must practice to become a successful real estate investor, the tips to change your mindset, and the misconceptions about generating passive income.

Increase Your Knowledge About Real Estate Investing

In this section, you will learn about the basics of flipping a property like what it means, the benefits it offers along with its drawbacks, the risks involved and how to mitigate those risks, steps for determining your goals and what you plan to achieve from real estate investing, and the ways to achieve your goals.

Understand the Secrets to Succeed in the Real Estate Industry

In this section, you will learn about some of the critical aspects of the real estate industry that will determine your success as an investor: the common manipulations you must watch out for, the way you can get the best possible deals on properties, and things you can do to ensure that you are taken seriously as an investor.

Find the Right Property to Invest In

Without the right property to invest in, you cannot become a successful investor. In this section, you will learn about all the people you need to hire: a property manager, real estate agent, a handyman, home inspector, and an attorney. You will learn about establishing a timeline while looking for a property, how and where to find flippable properties, different property options to choose from, laws involved, and other external factors.

Understand all the Aspects Involved in Viewing and Buying a Property

In this section, you will learn about the things you need to look for while analyzing a potential property you want to buy, about crunching numbers related to the property, the means to secure the necessary investing capital, different ratios to calculate, and the different negotiating tactics you can use to close a deal.

Steps to Start Making Money

To start earning money from the property, you need to increase the property's value. It means you must come up with cost-effective ways to increase your profit margin while ensuring you are getting your money's worth from the property and the services of contractors you use. In this section, you will learn about different things that must be improved prior to purchasing a property, the quick fixes you will need to make while flipping a property, whether to opt for a DIY approach or hire a contractor to help, negotiating with a contractor, and revamping the façade of the property in a cost-effective manner.

Have an Exit Strategy or a Backup Plan When Things Don't Go as Planned

A successful investor always has a plan B for when things go south. You must analyze the risk you are taking and have a backup plan you can put into action immediately when you feel like the market is turning unfavorable. Since you are interested in flipping houses, you need to know how to sell the property. In case you don't find any ideal buyers, you need to know what you can do to salvage your investment. You must know how to close a deal. Apart from this, you must be prepared for the worst-case scenario that all real estate investors dread - what do you do when things go wrong? If you fail to plan for all this, then you are setting yourself up for failure. You also need to be aware of the common mistakes to avoid while investing in real estate.

You will learn more about each of these steps in the subsequent chapters. By following these steps, you will be able to achieve financial independence and security while becoming a successful investor.

Section 2: Mindset + Lies

Chapter 4: The Lies of the 9-5

The reality of holding a 9-5 job is quite different from any expectations you might have about it. There are certain truths to it, which you must understand to evaluate your financial goals.

A 9-5 job eats away into one of your most precious assets: time. Time is a nonrenewable resource, and you must utilize it wisely. If you work all day long, it leaves you with little to no time to do the things you love.

Job security isn't something you can count on, and the fear of losing your job is quite real. Recession, a bad performance review, or even upsetting your boss can mean being handed the pink slip. You can lose your job for reasons that are almost always out of your control.

If you have any ideas of getting rich or retiring early, then a 9-5 job is not the way to attain it. The basic law of economics means that the worker only gets a wage while the entrepreneur receives all the profits. Your salary might increase from time to time, but that might not be sufficient to realize your financial goals.

The job hierarchy is just another reason for added stress. The lower you are placed in an organization's hierarchy, the greater your stress. You cannot be your own boss. You will always need to seek someone else's permission before you can do anything for something as simple as taking a day off. If you enjoy or crave autonomy, then you must reconsider your decision of holding onto a 9-5 job. The stress related to your job can affect other aspects of your life, like your physical and mental well-being. Typically, a 9-5 job encourages a sedentary lifestyle where you are stuck in a cubicle while working on a computer all day long. Such a lifestyle is extremely unhealthy.

If you want to be self-reliant, then you need to rethink your career goals. While working a 9-5 job, the only thing you can control is the way you work. Apart from this, you are at someone else's mercy all the time. So, if self-reliance is your goal, a 9-5 job will not help you achieve it.

It also creates a false sense of security. The idea of receiving a paycheck like clockwork is certainly comforting. After a while, this creates a sort of dependency on the paycheck, making it hard to think about anything else. If you want to succeed in life, you are going to have to step out of your comfort zone. However, a 9-5 job doesn't do this.

So, it is safe to say that job security is a thing of the past, and the only way to be secure is by becoming self-reliant. You need to add another source of income to your monthly earnings. The best way to do this is by investing in real estate.

Chapter 5: The Lie of Money

A lot of us believe certain myths about money, and this is mostly the result of societal conditioning. One of the most common misconceptions a lot of people seem to believe in is that "money is the root of all evil." You might have heard this phrase at some point in your life. Well, do you understand the dichotomy of this situation? On the one hand, we are all told from an early age that earning money is important, so we all work toward that goal. However, on the other hand, we are also led to believe that money is the cause of all evil.

If you believe this, then this thought will be stuck in your subconscious, and you might involuntarily shy away from all the chances you get to make money or might even try to get rid of it as quickly as you can, so you end up spending it all. You might also only think of those individuals who have earned money through unethical means, and it might make you believe that only the bad guys attain wealth.

For instance, let us assume that you have $1000 in your hands right now and you seem to think that the money you are holding is evil. If you believe something to be evil, the first thing you will want to do is get rid of it as quickly as you can. However, take a moment and think about it: "Is that paper you are holding evil?" That piece of paper has no power and is considered valuable only because of the value we assign to it.

The modern society we live in not only loves money and have money, but it also glorifies all those who have money. A lot of people seem to have made money their priority, and this is the main problem. Money is a resource that you have in life, but it doesn't encompass your entire life. The money will become evil only when you make it your sole priority and ignore everything else. For instance, think of a family of three, where both the parents are always at work to earn money. This means the family barely gets any time to spend together. Also, in their bid to chase money, they end up sacrificing a lot like mental peace, health, happiness, and family time. If you associate your happiness with earning money, then you will always be left unsatisfied.

So, money isn't the root of all evil, but being enamored with money is. The problem starts only when you obsess about money. When it comes to earning money, the journey matters more than the destination. When you adore money, you might think of all those who are rich and wish for all that they have at present, instead of thinking about all the struggles they went through to amass their wealth.

If you want to make money, stop daydreaming about money, and stop loving it. Instead, think about ways in which you can earn that money. You need dedication, hard work, commitment, and values to earn money.

Chapter 6: The Lie of Getting Rich Quick

Passive income sounds like a great way to make money. It essentially means setting up a source of income that will keep giving while freeing up your schedule to work on other things. There are several misconceptions about passive income and self-styled property gurus popularize most of these myths. Passive income refers to creating income by setting up an automated process that helps take care of the day-to-day operations of a business. However, a lot of people seem to believe that passive income refers to a business opportunity that helps generate income with little or even no effort. Well, that's just a lie, and you cannot allow yourself to fall for it. You cannot attain your goals without making the necessary effort, and this holds true for passive income too. Here are certain "get rich quick" myths about investing in real estate.

Myth #1: Learning Isn't Necessary

You cannot become a successful investor or even get started as one without knowing anything about real estate investing. Before you can buy a rental property, you must understand the different essential ratios and calculations including cash flow, the return on investment and internal rate of return and the capitalization rate. There is a learning curve, and you must be willing to learn to grow as an investor. You need to monitor the market trends, check any fluctuations in property prices, and soak in every bit of information you possibly can about real estate investing.

Myth #2: It is Quite Simple

Investing in real estate is presumed to be a piece of cake by a lot of newbie investors. If you thought there is no work involved in this form of investing, you need to think again. Be prepared to walk the extra mile to make sure you are getting a good deal on the property. You must work to find good property listings, analyze them, arrange the necessary capital, hire the necessary experts to help you along the way, and make the repairs to fix the property. You will need to manage the property, find potential sellers, and sell it. There are a lot of things involved, and you cannot skip any of these steps.

Myth #3: Less Effort

Your work doesn't end after buying the investment property. Maybe you can take a moment to breathe, but you certainly cannot relax right away. When flipping a house, you need to renovate the property, hire contractors for the same, work on your finances, ensure that the project is completed within the fixed time and budget, and only then can you sell it.

Fix-and-flip properties are also known as fixer-uppers, and these properties are for investors who are looking for an active source of income from short-term investments. Using the fixer-upper method, properties are acquired, renovated, and then sold. Don't think of it as a quick scheme that will make you rich. However, when done correctly, then the investor will profit from this particular strategy. When you are looking for a property to fix and flip, it is imperative to analyze all the deal-breakers. After setting a budget, you should probably contact an inspector, contractor, and assessor to identify potential time and money issues. Time is the most important asset when it comes to a coup. The longer it takes to turn a property over, the more expensive it becomes. The advantages of this strategy are that competition in the market is slightly lower. Not many people want to put their hands in the upper part. So you do not have to worry about big-time competition. In addition, you have complete autonomy in the redesign.

However, there are many risks associated with a fix-and-flip strategy. So you have to remember that your goal in this case is simple: to make money. You can't afford budget issues because it reduces your profits.

The main goal is to buy, repair and then sell a property at a profit. The main risk, however, would be to spend a lot of money on buying real estate and then spend even more on their repairs. The result will be expensive real estate that may be too expensive for this specific market.

You need to be realistic about profit if you want to avoid the risk of overcapitalization. You're probably out of luck selling a $1 million house in a reasonably priced area, where homes are usually sold for about $350,000 and the most expensive house is estimated at about $450,000. If your repair plan is complex, you should contact an experienced builder to help you with this process. It can make the difference between success and failure. Therefore, consider carefully before making a repair decision. Make sure your purchase agreement includes a pest control condition, as well. By inspecting buildings for pests, you can identify important deficiencies that can help you lower the price during negotiations. Also make sure that you have requested the approval of a local authority to begin the repairs.

It is impossible to deny that the costs of getting in and out of real estate investments are rather restrictive for many buyers. The costs include stamp duty, brokerage fees, advertising, any legal costs, mortgage costs and other costs associated with this process, all of which need to be included in the project budget.

Your profit equals the sales price less all costs incurred in repairing the property, the above costs and the purchase price. Take some time to calculate the entry and exit costs for each property you want to buy. This way, you can determine the specific property and its viability as an investment.

Chapter 7: How to Get Ahead

Awareness, networking, effort, and knowledge of the industry are all essential to success. However, it is as much about your mindset as it is about all these things. A change in your mindset can help accelerate your growth and improve your finances. Willpower and constant and consistent effort coupled with ambition can help change your mindset. You must adopt an abundance mindset if you want to be successful in life.

An abundance mindset is a change in your perception and attention. It is essentially about the resources available. An individual with an abundance mindset will truly believe that there are more than enough resources for not just themselves but others too. There is and will always be sufficient time, money, knowledge, and opportunities available. Having this mindset will help you succeed in the field of real estate investing. Here are some simple steps you can follow to develop this mindset.

Mindset About Scarcity

Scarcity doesn't necessarily have to be bad. There will be times when you might not have sufficient resources available. It might be in terms of labor, money, or even time. Instead of worrying about that scarcity, try to concentrate on things that you *can* control. Don't complain and instead take steps to rectify your situation. Complaining, whining, and moping around will not help you and will only lead to wasting more time. Instead, it is time to take action and fix the things you can.

Being Proactive

You must start anticipating and not just wait. Waiting is a passive act wherein you aren't involved, whereas anticipation helps generate excitement and expectation. When you anticipate something, you will be better prepared to deal with things. Instead of worrying about failure, wake up in the morning anticipating success. If you are flipping a house at the moment, anticipate all the things that can potentially go wrong and come up with strategies to deal with or even avoid them altogether. By doing this, you will ensure that you are always prepared and will never be caught off-guard.

Don't Procrastinate

Don't let procrastination get ahold of you. Make it your priority to do things as and when needed instead of putting them off for later. If something needs to be done now, do it immediately. You might not want to work on something at the moment, but the more you delay it, the lesser will your motivation be to get that work done.

Company Matters

The company you keep influences the way you think. When you surround yourself with motivated, passionate, happy, and ambitious people, their positive traits are bound to rub off on you too. Keeping negative company will only fester more negativity. Take some time and analyze all the relationships in your life and practically consider whether any of them are holding you back. It is better to get rid of the negative connections instead of letting them hold you back.

Believe in Yourself

At the risk of sounding cocky, it is important that you believe you are unique. No, this doesn't make you a narcissist; it is about learning to appreciate who you are and what you can do. You are a unique individual and you can use that knowledge to your advantage. Embrace your personality, both the positives and negatives. Only when you acknowledge and embrace your flaws will you be able to turn them into strengths.

Changing your mindset will take some time, and you need to work on it daily. Start maintaining a gratitude journal to make a list of all the things you are grateful for and jot down all the victories you achieve, regardless of how big or small they are. Learning to be positive and motivated will give you the necessary willpower to keep going. Spend some time listening to or watching inspirational videos like TED Talks, surround yourself with positive people, and take some time out for self-care.

Chapter 8: Creature of Habit

You cannot achieve success overnight, and you must be prepared to take small steps every day to get the success you want. In this section, you will learn about a couple of simple things you can do each day to change your mindset and create helpful habits on the road to becoming successful.

Planning

Planning is essential for every aspect of your life, and the same applies to real estate investing too. You must set some short-term and long-term goals and work towards achieving them. To do this, you need a business plan that will allow you to visualize and concentrate on your goals instead of focusing on any setbacks you face. Real estate investing is certainly demanding, and if you have a solid plan of action, it will help you stay focused and organized.

Learn About the Market

You must thoroughly understand the market you are investing in. You must stay updated about all the different trends and changes taking place in the market like the spending habits of consumers, mortgage rates, and changes in real estate valuation, to name a few. It helps you plan for the future and make the necessary changes. Being prepared helps increase your chances of being successful.

Be Ethical

There are no specific ethics that a real estate investor needs to abide by. It might seem like you can easily take advantage of such situations, but a successful investor knows the importance of maintaining ethical standards. Real estate investing involves other people, so your reputation matters. If you stay ethical, it helps improve your reputation.

Niche

You need to focus on one specific niche to gain in-depth knowledge about it in order to become successful. No one can possibly be aware of everything in every arena. So, select a niche and take some time to develop a thorough understanding of that niche to become successful.

Stay Up to Date

It is essential that you stay abreast of all the changes and latest trends in laws, terminology, and regulations related to the world of real estate investing. If you fall behind, then you won't just lose your momentum in the market but might also find yourself in unnecessary legal trouble.

Consider the Risks

Regardless of the investment option you opt for, there will always be certain risks involved with it. You must understand the different risks of real estate investing. Only when you are aware of the risks will you be able to mitigate those risks and make smart decisions. Being prudent is a very important skill for any real estate investor. Make sure that you are aware and understand all the risks involved, not only with real estate deals themselves but all the legal implications they pose, and adjust your investment strategy to reduce these risks.

Hire Help

Hire help whenever you feel like there is something you cannot do by yourself. If crunching numbers isn't your strong suit, then hire an accountant to do it for you. Before you seek professional help, spend some time understanding the basic aspects of the business that they will help you with. It is okay to seek assistance, but blindly depending on someone is not a good idea.

Networking

You must think about networking and work toward establishing your network. A good network can give you support, along with the opportunities necessary to become a successful investor. Your network can consist of business partners, your clients, contractors you work with, building managers, real estate agents, or anyone else who can help you along the way.

Section 3: Increase your Knowledge

Chapter 9: Let's Start at the Beginning

Flipping is an investment strategy wherein the investor will purchase an asset and then sell it for a profit instead of holding it on a long-term basis or waiting for long-term appreciation. Flipping is commonly used to denote all short-term real estate transactions with the intent of selling it fast. In real estate, flipping can be divided into two categories. In the first type, a real estate investor will target such properties whose market value is appreciating quickly and then resell the property with little to no extra investment in improving the physical property. This technique relies on market conditions instead of the property. If the market is favorable, you stand to gain a lot by doing this. The second method of flipping is where the investor buys a property, makes changes to the property or renovates the property based on the potential buyer's needs, and then sells it.

A common mentality that a lot of investors have, regardless of the type of investment, is the "buy low and sell high" mentality. As the name suggests, it means that you must try to buy the property at as low a cost as you possibly can and then resell it when the market is favorable to earn greater profits. Earning profits will be one of your major goals as an investor. However, you need to be careful while following this mentality. If you hold the property for too long before selling it, you stand to lose out on your investment. So, to avoid falling into this trap, you must evaluate the historical data about the market conditions, the predictions for the future, consider your finances, and make a decision accordingly. You don't always have to go with the market trend, but it is a good idea to stay prudent.

There are several benefits of flipping a property, and we will discuss them below.

Profitability

Flipping a property is a great way to make a quick profit, and this is one of the main reasons why a lot of people enter this market. However, this is possible only when you follow a flipping strategy properly. You can earn a profit on a property by flipping it and selling it within a couple of months, provided the market conditions stay favorable.

Gain Experience

Flipping properties is a great way to gain a lot of experience in the real estate industry. It teaches you about different aspects of real estate like construction because of the likely renovation, repairs, and any remodeling work you might have to undertake to appreciate the property's value and make it more appealing to potential buyers. You will learn about spotting any structural issues and all the costs involved in these processes. It will help you learn about the local market since the first thing you must do before flipping a property is to find the ideal property. To do this, you will need to spend some time researching the local market and get an idea of the requirements of your potential buyers. Once you place the flipped property up for sale, it will help you gain insight into the mindset and the requirements of the buyers in a specific area. You can use these insights to make the necessary changes in the next property you want to flip. Theoretical and practical knowledge are quite different. You might have read everything there is to know about real estate investing. However, only when you get into the field and start "getting your hands dirty" will you truly learn about it. Flipping will teach you about any unexpected costs you can incur like building permits, delays in receiving the permits and clearances, or even any disputes with contractors.

Helps With Networking

Flipping will help in increasing your network. When you undertake the job of flipping a property, you will invariably end up making a lot of connections with different people involved in the industry like contractors, lawyers, realtors, insurance agents, building inspectors, other investors, and even accountants. It is essential to keep all these contacts since they can come in handy later.

Personal Satisfaction

Another benefit of real estate flipping is that it gives you a chance to see a vision that only a few others can. When you are flipping a property, you are not judging it for what it is at present. Instead, you can see the potential it offers which others couldn't. By doing this, it will give you a sense of personal pride that will give you the motivation to keep going.

Myths About Flipping

Regardless of the popularity of flipping, there are certain myths about this industry. Here are all the popular myths about flipping properties.
A lot of people seem to think that it is a quick and easy job to flip a property. How hard can it be to buy a property, renovate or fix it, and then sell it? It might sound straightforward, but completing these steps will take a lot of time, energy, and resources. When you plan to flip a property, it is essential that you set certain realistic and achievable goals for yourself, which you can attain within a fixed time and budget. If you are unsure of how long it will take, don't hesitate to seek help.

If you have watched any episodes of *Fixer Upper* or any other similar reality flipping TV shows, then it might make you believe that the concept of a "dud" property doesn't exist. Giving a house a makeover or making repairs is not an easy process, It takes a lot of dedication, skill, time, motivation, and money. It might seem like you can sell a fixer-upper for a huge profit, but before you can sell it, you need to flip the house. Also, the profitability quotient depends on external factors like the economic climate, local market conditions, buyer sentiments in the market, demand, and financing options available. Unless all these conditions are favorable, you cannot make a huge profit as you hoped. So, before you decide to purchase a property, you must do all the necessary research and homework about the market you choose. You must also evaluate the other factors that can influence the property's value during and after the completion of flipping the property.

You need a sound plan to attain the goal of flipping a property within a fixed time and budget. As with any task, there are chances of the costs increasing while flipping a project. Costs aren't always easy to control, and you need to ensure that you leave a little wiggle room while setting the budget. Also, make it a point to consider all the possible costs that will crop up and include them in the budget, regardless of how minor they seem.

People seem to think that drama is restricted to soap operas. Oh, boy, are they wrong! Watching drama on reality television is quite interesting, but it can also be something you might have to deal with while flipping a property yourself. Flipping a property can be an anxiety-inducing and stressful project. It might become difficult to stick to a budget, timeline, or even both. Apart from this, there can be differences in opinions, and butting heads can be fairly common. So, please be prepared for some drama and ensure that you have the necessary patience to deal with this. Always keep a plan in place for the renovation as well as for the resolution of any potential conflicts. By doing this, you can ensure that the process of flipping the property will go as smoothly as possible.

Chapter 10: Risks

As with any other form of investment, there are certain risks involved in flipping properties too, and we will discuss some of them here.

Market Trends

One of the obvious risks you have to watch out for is market trends. What direction is the market moving in? Is it headed toward a boom, is it stable, or will it crash? Ensure that you evaluate the past trends along with the current trends to understand the market conditions.

Shift in Demographics

There can always be a shift in the demographics of your area. Your ideal demographic can grow or decline. This shift usually determines your pricing strategies. Use the data provided by different online sources to analyze the local demographics.

Interest Rates

If you take a loan or a mortgage to purchase the property, then ensure that you keep a record of the interest rates. If the interest rates increase, it will increase your capital requirements and can also eat into your profit margins.

Evaluation

When you decide to close on a potential deal, you need to evaluate it. Valuation of a property involves determining the likely selling price, the after repair value or ARV, and the analysis of return on investment. Hire the services of an appraiser to get the ARV appraisal for any property rehab plans you have. Get multiple opinions if you aren't sure of the valuation of the property. This helps you decide whether to buy a specific property or not. If you don't buy it at the right price and the right time, you stand to lose more than you gain.

Lack of Knowledge

As you get started, you might be tempted to do everything by yourself so that you understand how the entire process works. The major problem this poses is that you might not have all the necessary skills and tools to get the job done. This, in turn, can increase your costs, waste your time, and even lead to unnecessary frustration. The best thing to do is to find the ideal equipment and hire professionals to do the work for you.
Flipping houses might be a new area to venture in. When entering a new field, you must be aware of all that it encompasses, so you make wise decisions. Flipping a property can become an expensive gamble if you aren't careful. So, the best thing to do is gain more experience to get a feel of what you need to do.

Hidden Repairs

Hidden repairs are rather common when it comes to flipping properties. You might discover some repairs that are necessary while renovating a property that you were earlier totally unaware of. So, it is absolutely essential that you spend the necessary time and do the research to consider all the repairs you might have to undertake. By ignoring certain costs, you only increase the risks with your investment.

Chapter 11: What Do You Want Out of Life?

Well, now that you are aware of the different benefits flipping houses offers and the risks you need to be aware of, it is time to identify your investment goals. So, what are your reasons for investing in real estate? Failure to plan means you are planning to fail. Without an end goal in mind, you will not get very far in life, and this holds true for real estate investment too.

Having a goal lends a sense of purpose, regardless of what you want to do. So, why are you investing? The reasons to invest will certainly vary from one person to the next. Without a goal, you cannot plan, and without a plan, you cannot expect the odds to be favorable. Without these things, the investment you want to make might not do you any good.

Why do you need to set a goal? A goal will not only keep you motivated when obstacles crop up, but it also helps analyze whether the investment you want to make will be profitable or not. It will come in handy while estimating your budget, the possible risks, and the returns you want.

Before you can think about investing, think about your investment goals. Are you investing in creating an additional source of income? Do you want to save for retirement? Do you like the idea of having a passive source of income? Do you want to save for your child's future, or do you have any other goal in mind? By understanding your motivation for investing, you can make better decisions.

Take a while and think about all your reasons. Once you have these reasons in mind, it is time to divide them into different categories. Separate your goals into long-term and short-term goals. For instance, a short-term goal might be to save for a luxurious vacation, and a long-term goal might be to create a retirement nest egg for yourself. Take the time to make a note of these goals - don't just rely on a mental list. When you write your goals down, you have to review those goals regularly, and it will provide the necessary motivation to keep going.

While setting goals, there is a simple acronym you can use, and that's *SMART* goals. The goals you set must be *specific*, *measurable*, *achievable*, *realistic*, and *time-bound*. If the goal you set meets all these requirements, then the chances of attaining it increase dramatically.

Specific

The goal you set must be specific; a vague goal doesn't make any sense. For instance, if you want to create a retirement fund, then your goal cannot just be "create a retirement fund." This goal is too vague, and when the goal is vague, it gives you leeway to procrastinate. A specific goal would be "I want to save $50,000 for retirement by 2021."

Measurable

The next step is to ensure that the goals you set are measurable. You can attach a monetary value to your investment goal and you can measure your progress. For instance, if you are saving for a luxurious vacation in Greece, then you might need about $15,000 per week. By attaching a monetary value to the goal, it becomes more real.

Attainable

The goal needs to be achievable. If the goal is impossible to achieve, you will be in for nothing but disappointment. For instance, a goal like "I want to make all the repairs and do the renovation work by myself" is unachievable if you do not know how to perform any repair work.

Realistic

The goal must be realistic. For instance, a goal like "I want to flip this property within a week and sell it" is unrealistic. Not only does it take time to flip a property, but it takes some time to find an ideal buyer too.

Time-bound

The goal needs to be time-bound. When you set a deadline, it increases your motivation to work and reduces the chances of procrastination. So, ensure that you give yourself a realistic deadline for attaining your goal.

Chapter 12: Why You Should Do It Anyway

Investing in real estate certainly does have certain risks, but the benefits it offers outweigh those risks. Life isn't always peachy, and neither is investing, and that's perfectly normal. By learning to keep yourself motivated, regardless of all that's happening in life, you can move on. There will be good and bad days in investing too. So, how can you ensure that you have the motivation to keep going even when you feel like it is an impossibly difficult uphill battle? Here are certain tips you can use to change your attitude and keep yourself motivated.

Positive Thinking

The power of positive thinking cannot be underestimated. Start practicing positive affirmations daily to keep up your spirits. If you ever feel overwhelmed, a little low on energy, or demotivated, then positive affirmations can help heal your spirit. Take a couple of minutes daily, forget about everything else, and concentrate on yourself. You can use positive affirmations like "I am capable of attaining my goals," "Every obstacle I face is a learning experience," or "Each day, I am a step closer to my goals." Feel free to come up with any positive affirmations you like. Here is a simple exercise you can follow.
Find a peaceful spot for yourself, close your eyes, and breathe in slowly. Repeat the positive affirmation of your choice. Exhale slowly and repeat this process. Do this until your mind feels a little lighter. Once you open your eyes, you will notice that the negative voice in your head is feebler and you can get on with your day.

Surround Yourself With Positivity

The company you keep influences the way you think and feel. So, make it a point to surround yourself with positive people. Notice the company you keep and the general vibe they give out. Start to listen to all those you surround yourself with. Do they give out positive vibes, or does it feel like all they do is complain or whine? Do they encourage you to do better, or do they hold you back?

Did you ever look at crabs in a pot? The ones at the bottom of the pot tend to pull down all the crabs that are at the top trying to get out of the pot. Likewise, by surrounding yourself with negative people who sap your energy, you can feel demotivated. Have a positive outlook in life and surround yourself with positive people.

Vision Journal

You can maintain a vision journal. The concept is quite simple: make a list of your goals and find any images that describe or relate to your goal and paste them in a book. Fill the book with a list of things you are grateful for and a list of things you want to achieve. Whenever you feel low on energy, take some time and go through your vision book.

To-do List

Keep track of the tasks you need to achieve and a timeframe within which you must complete them. Essentially, you need to make to-do lists. Making a list helps measure your progress and will leave you with a sense of accomplishment upon completing the tasks assigned for the day. It will give you a sense of purpose along with a sense of direction. Before you go to sleep at night, take some time and make a list of tasks for the next day. This way, as soon as you wake up on the following morning, you will be keenly aware of all the things you must accomplish. Also, this is a great way to overcome procrastination.

Comfort Zone

If you want to be successful, you need to step out of your comfort zone. Staying in your comfort zone is certainly reassuring, and it might make you feel secure. However, success seldom lies within your comfort zone. At times, especially when you are facing any challenges, you might feel like not doing anything. If you ever feel like this, then the worst thing you can do is not act. When you feel low or overwhelmed by things, do something out of the ordinary. It can be something as simple as going on a leisurely walk after dinner to clear your head. Make it a point to keep learning every single day.

Section 4: The Secrets They Don't Want You to Know

Chapter 13: Summary of the Real Estate Industry in 2019

Regardless of whether you want to buy or sell, here are a couple of trends in the real estate market in 2019.

The first trend observed in the market is that the prices of property are slowly increasing. During 2017 and the first portion of 2018, the prices of housing properties increased by around 10%. It is predicted that the prices of housing properties are set to increase in 2019 too, but at a slower pace. This slowdown is because of the increase in rates of mortgage interest coupled with economic uncertainty. This combination of factors is discouraging new buyers from entering the market.

This doesn't mean there are no buyers in the market, though. The construction of newly constructed properties is steadily increasing. So, if you are looking forward to selling a property this year, you might make a good profit on the sale. Since the number of buyers isn't too large this year, you must ensure that you do everything to make your property better than the rest. You must become aware of your competition in the market, price the property accordingly, and ensure that it has certain features that will appeal to your potential buyers.

There has been a steady increase in the rates of mortgage interest. The common trend observed in mortgage interest rates is that they tend to increase after being almost constant. The interest rates are set to go up, and it has been about seven years since mortgage prices were this high. The mortgage interest on 15-year and 30-year mortgages is set to increase by 4.4 and 5% respectively. These measures are being enacted to help stabilize the economy and fight rising inflation. The Federal Reserve increased the rates of interest on short-term loans. All this essentially means that people are not only willing to spend but are willing to borrow too. As a seller, you might have to prepare to have your house on the market for a while longer, and there might be a decline in the number of offers you receive.

A lot of the buyers in the real estate market are millennials. Millennials are gradually overtaking the homeowner leaderboard. The market estimates show that this year, a majority of the mortgages will be held by millennials, followed by gen Xers and baby boomers. So, what does this trend mean in the real estate market? When it comes to millennials, you must work on a very important concept to become successful at flipping houses. You must make an effort to understand your buyers. Millennials tend to look online before making their purchases, to ensure that as a potential seller, you must make your properties look fetching on the Internet. Quality matters more than square footage to this generation of buyers. So, ensure that the space you want to sell will appeal to millennials. Another thing you must consider while investing in a property is its location.

If you are neither interested in buying or selling a property this year, here is what you must be aware of right now.

The rate of equity is set to increase at a rate between 2 to 6% per annum until 2020. This is certainly great news for sellers, but even if you aren't selling, your equity is set to increase. You might think that the real estate market is headed for a crash because of the increase in mortgage interest rates. Well, you don't have to worry about this because the economy is going to stay strong for the foreseeable future. There has been an increase in general spending, the unemployment rate is low, and taxes are low too.

Chapter 14: Secrets of the Real Estate Industry

Here are the secrets about the real estate industry you need to be aware of. These secrets will not only help sell your property quickly but will also ensure that you are getting your money's worth from your real estate agent.

About Open Houses

Open houses were effective in the past, but not anymore. In the past, if you wanted to sell a property, then the only means through which potential buyers could view the property was through open houses. Well, these days, if a buyer has to see a property, they can easily view them online on different websites from the comfort of their own homes. If your real estate agent insists on hosting an open house, it is only a tactic to obtain new clients for themselves who might be looking to sell their properties. So, don't bother yourself with the hassle of hosting an open house.

A Good Agent is Necessary

As a fixer-upper, you will need to sell the flipped property to make money. If you want to sell a property, then the one reason you must hire a real estate agent is to help with marketing. An agent good at their job can help you get qualified buyers for the property and do so quickly so that you can get the best possible price on the property. Marketing is essential to becoming successful in the business of real estate. Here are certain things you must be aware of while hiring a realtor.

Whenever you are hiring someone to sell a property, ensure that the person you want to hire is a qualified Realtor. There is a difference between a real estate agent and a Realtor. A Realtor can list your property in the MLS (a database of homes available for sale) while a real estate agent cannot. The Realtor must understand about marketing and must be proactive while helping you market the property. Don't get tricked into believing that if an agent works for a big firm, your property will get more views online.

Discount Brokers

Opting for discount brokers or limited services brokers isn't necessarily a bad idea. Regardless of the popular opinion in the real estate industry, hiring the services of such brokers is a good idea in two specific situations. The first one is if you have a property for under $120,000. Why should you hire limited services or a discount broker? Well, an agent will only receive a commission on the selling price of the property. For instance, if the house is priced at $120,000, the listing commission is 3%, the firm's split of the listing commission is 35$, the estimated taxes payable by the agent is 25%, and the marketing costs are about $800. Let's crunch some numbers now.

When you calculate all this, the agent only gets $640 in hand at the end of closing the deal. Well, the services provided by the agent will depend on the amount they stand to earn. Keep this in mind while hiring an agent. If this is the case, then you can save yourself a couple of hundred dollars by hiring discount brokers.

The second scenario where you can use the services of discount brokers is when the property market is hot. The market is set to be hot when the demand for properties is readily met with supply, and in fact, the demand surpasses the supply. If that's the overall climate in the real estate market, then it becomes easy to sell a property. If you are aware that there are buyers readily available in the market, then all that you have to do is be cost-effective and hire the services of a discount broker.

As with any other industry, there is a lot of competition within the real estate industry. A lot of investors seem to think that all agents are created equal. Well, that's not the case. There might be some who offer better service and might charge a higher fee. However, it doesn't mean that the costliest agent you can hire is the best fit for you. You have to ensure that you carefully interview the agent before deciding to use their services.

Chapter 15: The Most Common Ways the Real Estate Industry Takes Advantage of You

The real estate market is not immune to fraud and other investment scams. It can be in the form of a fraudulent contractor who charges exorbitant fees and doesn't do any work, or it might even be an investment agent who outright embezzles your hard-earned money. You must protect yourself from these scams by being vigilant and doing the necessary homework before jumping into this industry. Here are the common ways in which the real estate industry can take advantage of you.

Title fraud can be a major setback for property owners, and it usually starts with identity theft. The scammer might falsify the documents and pose as a property owner, register all the forged documents and transfer the property to himself, and claim a new mortgage against the property. Once the mortgage is secured, the scammer will take the money and disappear while the homeowner is now left with a hefty mortgage.

Another means through which title fraud is committed is by fraudulently selling a property without the proper title. So, you must ensure that you carefully check whether the seller has the title documents to make the sale and everything is in order.

You can avoid this by taking out title insurance that will protect you from title fraud. Not only will this safeguard the new owner from all existing liens on the property, but it will also protect them from encroachment issues. Another simple way to protect yourself from fraud is by being cautious while sharing your information with others.

Be wary of any creative descriptions that seem tempting. Remember that using a creative description is seldom anything more than a marketing tactic. Well, if the real estate agent tells you mature trees surround the property, it might not necessarily mean a beautiful canopy and might mean old trees that need to be pruned immediately, or worse - diseased trees. When the agent says the house has plenty of potential, the potential the agent is referring to might mean a lot of repairs just to make it inhabitable. Always make it a point to visit the properties instead of relying on the descriptions you are given.

At times, properties available for sale are listed "as is." This is another manipulative tactic used to sell a property with physical defects that might not clear the necessary structural or mechanical inspections. When a property is listed "as is," it means the seller doesn't make any guarantees whatsoever about the condition of the property. This is considered to be the "Hail Mary" a seller uses to get rid of the property. You must stay away from all these listings if you want to flip houses and gain profits.

As mentioned earlier, the agent only receives a commission on the house sold. The commission received is split between the real estate agency or firm and the agent. So, don't be surprised if all the listings given to you by the agent aren't in your price range. This is being done to increase the agent's earnings instead of meeting your needs.

Another manipulative tactic used is upselling. This is a practice of showing the potential buyer only such properties that are slightly above their ideal price range. If your agent is doing this, it might make you feel like your budget is too low. All that the agent is doing is fattening their paycheck. It will encourage overspending unnecessarily to increase your costs.

If the property market is hot and you are buying a property, then it is highly likely that you will face some competition; however, if the property has been listed for a couple of months and if the agent tells you there is a competitive offer on the same, be wary. This is usually used to deceive potential buyers into closing a deal quickly.

Agents also tend to manipulate sales comparisons. Whenever a house is listed, the agent will usually make a compilation of the market analysis so that you can compare the listed property against the value of similar properties that were recently sold. This usually helps determine the selling price of the property. However, if the agent manipulates these prices, then it might make it seem like the property is worth way more than it is.

Another common tactic is to focus only on the location. The properties shown to you might be in a wonderful location, but the property price might be too high. If that's the case, then you might be tempted into buying something you cannot afford.

These manipulative tactics are often used to con a buyer, and you must be wary of them. The best way to protect yourself from such tactics is by showing that you are a serious investor. You will learn more about this in the next chapter.

Chapter 16: How to Be Taken Seriously as a First-Time Buyer

Appearances can go a long way, and this is especially true for all first-time buyers who are just entering the real estate industry. Here are some simple ways in which you can make others in the industry take you seriously.

Knowledge Matters

There is nothing that can substitute knowledge. Successful investors always seem to know what they are doing and their reasons for doing it. A real estate investor with a diverse and large portfolio usually knows more about the market, the forces that guide the market, about timing market cycles, and also the things to be wary of. They are likely to recognize any changes that take place in the market before others seem to. All these things make them more successful than other investors in the market.

So, what makes them good? They are successful because they never stop learning. There are different resources you can use to increase your knowledge about investing in real estate. There are different online forums, websites, and blogs you can use to keep up to date with the market.

Here are certain skills you need to develop if you want to come across as a knowledgeable investor. You must learn to analyze the cash flow of a property.

The ability to recognize when the property is over- or undervalued.

Learn about the different economic and external factors that influence the market.

Learn about the different aspects involved with flipping properties.

By learning these basic skills, you can rely on your judgment instead of on someone else's. The chances of others trying to manipulate you will reduce drastically when you seem knowledgeable about the industry.

Patience

You must learn to have patience. It might sound like a very simple skill, but it isn't always easy to be patient. When you are investing in real estate, there is usually a lot of pressure placed on having to act fast. The best deals on the market are gone within the blink of an eye. This means that investors are constantly under pressure to think and decide quickly.

You cannot ignore this pressure, but you can certainly learn to deal with it. The best thing to do is ensure that you don't let this pressure get to you and wait to see how things progress. Patience is a much-needed virtue in all aspects of life, and real estate investing isn't any exception. You can avoid making costly mistakes by being patient. Patience often comes in different forms in the real estate industry. By learning to identify the areas wherein you must be patient, it can save you from getting into unnecessary trouble. A common and often costly mistake a lot of investors make is that they invest in a property only because it might help them meet the goal they have set in their minds.

A lot of newbies set deadlines within which they need to invest in their next property, and this makes them feel pressured into meeting the deadline. It might mean compromising on certain things and investing in a deal that might not be all that great. A good investor knows that it isn't the number of deals, but the *quality* of deals they close that matters. It is better to be patient and wait for the right deals to come along instead of investing in any property that comes their way out of desperation.

Another common problem that a lot of new investors make is that they tend to start in the unfavorable part of the market cycle. It might be tempting to purchase when you see other investors buying. However, a successful investor knows that it isn't always a good idea to follow the market trends. Avoid doing anything just because others seem to be doing it. Instead, jump in only when you need to and things are favorable. Dealing with the pressure and learning to be patient is a fine skill to develop, so work on it.

See the Potential

At least superficially, investing in real estate might seem like a numbers game, but that's seldom the case. When flipping a property, you will end up buying a property and making changes or improvements to it, which will help the property's value appreciate. So, it means you must be able to see the potential in the property along with the returns it can generate. You must be able to see what you can attain by acquiring a property. A common phrase used in real estate is "highest and best use." It denotes the idea of finding the best possible use for the property and working to attain that outcome. A good investor understands this concept.

It isn't just about finding good deals, but the ability to *make* good deals that matters too. By having a realistic vision for the property, even a novice investor comes across as a serious investor. Since you are interested in flipping a property, it will do you good to have certain ideas for flipping the property like renovating the interiors, doing up the external façade, working on the landscaping, and basic plumbing upgrades. These things will help increase the value of the property too.

Efficiency

Efficiency is a skill that is indispensable in all aspects of life, and real estate investing is no different. A lot of us can accomplish more than what we do if we could work efficiently and reduce any distractions. A top investor is quite good in this area.

To become efficient, you must be able to identify those things that take up a lot of your time and don't contribute to your bottom line. By streamlining your daily life and coming up with ways to automate mundane tasks like replying to emails, you can save a lot of time. By doing this, it frees up a lot of your time that you can spend on other, more meaningful tasks. Once you become efficient, it makes it easier to demand the best from those around you. It reduces the chances of contractors missing out on their deadlines when they are aware that their boss is efficient and expects the same from them. A successful investor knows to lead by example. When you are efficient in your dealings, you can expect the same from others, and this will keep others on their toes. All these things help improve your overall productivity.

Unwavering Focus

Another trait that differentiates a novice investor from a veteran is their focus. Obstacles are common, and they slow you down, but it doesn't mean they are the end of the road. A light bulb can brighten up a room, but the bulb's energy is dispersed. However, a laser is highly focused, and its energy is concentrated. A laser can go through obstacles that stop a light bulb. A successful investor has a laser-sharp focus. They don't let any obstacles stop them, and they are quite aware of the direction they are headed in and their goal. You must not only know what you need to achieve, and the work others need to do to help you along the way, but you must also know how to avoid any unnecessary distractions.

Networking

There is another common feature that all successful business people share, and it is that they are good at networking. Networking can make all the difference between being a so-so investor and a successful one. Relationship building and networking are often overlooked skills. Don't underestimate the value of networking. It can mean getting the best pricing for renovation work, getting a better response when the need arises, and it might even mean getting to know about the best deals on properties. You might have heard the phrase, "It is not about what you know, but who you know that matters?" A successful investor doesn't deny this fact and embraces it with open arms.

Having a list of contractors, handymen, law enforcement officers, accountants, lawyers, and real estate agents is an invaluable asset. Having someone to call when the need arises can save you a lot of time, effort, and energy. If you want to build relationships, then you need to offer value to others in order to obtain value from them.

Leverage

The final trait all successful real estate investors possess is their ability to use leverage. You must learn to leverage people, money, and opportunities. There will always come a time wherein an investor might have more deals and opportunity than the capital available with them. At such instances, the skill to use other people's money (and repaying them) is the best way to scale your investments. By leveraging the resources that others have, you can grow the size of your portfolio and your wealth along the way. This means it creates a win-win situation that benefits those you partner with too.

You must learn to leverage other people too. It can be in the form of hiring hard-working, skilled, and trustworthy people and partnering with the right people. One of the common mistakes a novice investor may make is to try and do everything by themselves. If you want to flip properties successfully, then you must learn to leverage the skills and talents of others and use those to your advantage.

One final thing that you must learn to leverage is opportunity. Successful business people know that every win is more than just a victory; it is a chance for another opportunity later on. Whenever you complete a project successfully, you can use that success as leverage for your next project. The contacts you make along the way, and the experience you gain while doing one thing can be leveraged later. When you work on renovating and flipping a property, you can use the experience you gain from it to work more effectively and efficiently on any future projects.

FBI Negotiation Tactics

There are certain tactics used by trained FBI agents during negotiations, and you can use these tactics while negotiating deals in the real estate industry too. Here are all the skills you can use.

The first skill you must develop is to start listening actively. Active listening is quite different from just hearing the words being said. It is about listening to what the speaker says and ensuring that you make the speaker know that you are listening carefully. Everyone likes to feel heard, and with active listening, you can easily establish a better rapport with the other person. For instance, if you are negotiating a deal with a potential seller, it would be ideal to have a good rapport with them in order to negotiate a better deal.

The next thing you need to do is build that rapport. Once you understand the motives and objectives of the person you are negotiating with, you can plan your responses such that it resonates with their objectives and their thinking. This might seem like manipulation, but it isn't.

Negotiation is a two-way street, and when you think about it, it is like a two-player game. FBI agents are trained at Quantico, and one of the things they are taught is hostage negotiation. An FBI negotiator knows the importance of negotiation and is aware that it is all about using emotional intelligence.

Section 5: Finding the Right House

Chapter 17: The Dream Team

Flipping properties is not a solo act and is like a well-coordinated symphony. As with any orchestra, you must develop it one instrument after the other, and this happens through networking. To build a good orchestra, you need to participate in the real estate investing community actively. Before you can start flipping a property, you must have a "dream team" in place that will help you attain your goals. The "dream team" essentially consists of different professionals you must hire to assist you in different areas of the flipping process. Your team must include a real estate attorney, an accountant, an insurance agent, contractor, and a real estate agent.

Real Estate Attorney

You get what you pay for, and this holds true for the real estate attorney you hire. Most people know that this is true but it isn't often that they pay it any heed. For instance, if you purchase a cheap shirt from a shady roadside vendor, it is likely that it will fall apart within a couple of washes. Similarly, when you are hiring an attorney to help with your real estate transactions, you must ensure that you are hiring someone who knows what they are doing. A good attorney plays a critical role in helping you become a successful real estate investor. Hiring an attorney worth their salt might seem like an expensive bill initially, but it will be worth the costs you incur. Instead of having to spend a lot of money later for any legal troubles, it is better to hire a good lawyer who will help avoid all such mistakes. Hiring an unskilled or unqualified attorney will only increase your operating costs. Before you start transacting in real estate, you need an attorney and don't make the mistake of acting on your own unless you have a thorough understanding of the laws related to real estate. You will need a real estate attorney because a real estate agent isn't qualified to assist you with legal issues like zoning troubles, environmental concerns, township ordinances, or any other restrictions that can influence the ownership or use of the property. An attorney will help you with any transactions that involve boundary disputes, estate sales, or even survey issues that can complicate a transaction. You can also use the services of an attorney while reviewing any loan or financial documents to ensure that you fully understand your obligations and rights.

CPA

You will need a certified public accountant (or CPA) to help you with managing all the accounting work related to flipping properties. You might think that you are well versed with tax laws, but it is always wise to have a good CPA who is aware of the different expenses which can be deducted, the assets which can be capitalized, and other such nuances you might not have a thorough understanding of. Laws tend to change frequently, and keeping up with them can become tiring. If you hire a CPA, you don't have to worry about all this and can rest easy knowing that a skilled professional is taking care of your books of accounts and filing the necessary tax returns on time.

Insurance Agent

Insurance is another major aspect of flipping properties. As mentioned above, it isn't likely that you are aware of all the nuances of insurance. The insurance agent you include in the flipping team must have a thorough understanding of all the different technical aspects of your business structure, the details about the properties which must be insured, the kind of insurance you need to take on and they must be able to give you sound advice related to all aspects of insurance. Houses that are being flipped need several kinds of insurance that a regular buy-and-hold property doesn't. Remember that the team you hire is like an orchestra and you must act as the conductor of that orchestra. Instead of trying to do everything on your own, hire some professional help. "A stitch in time saves nine" is the best way to think when hiring professionals.

Contractors

There will be a lot of renovation, construction, and repair work you will need to undertake while flipping houses. The best option is to hire contractors to help you with all this instead of trying to do it all yourself. As with any other member of the team you hire, you must find the best contractor, one whom you can trust and depend on. Every state has different rules and regulations about contractors and ensures that you are aware of the different qualifications a licensed contractor must possess. When you hire a contractor, ensure that you check their bond and insurance, as well as licenses. Apart from this, check their ID to verify that the contractor is licensed in the state you live. Also, ask for any previous references to crosscheck the contractor's reliability. A contractor is essentially responsible for all the rehab work you undertake while flipping a property along with hiring and managing the other members of the subcontracting team like handymen, plumbers, electricians, roofers, drywallers, property managers, and carpenters to get the job done.

Real Estate Agent

The final member of your team is a real estate agent. A qualified estate agent will help you not only buy a property but also its resale. You might work with multiple real estate agents, but it is a good idea to limit the number of agents you work with. You might also want to use the services of different agents according to the services you need. For instance, an REO or a real estate owned agent focuses only on short sales. A short sale is one where the sale of the property will "fall short" of any existing debts against that property. Such agents usually work with banks and financial institutions to help the seller sell a property before the property is foreclosed. Carefully interview the potential real estate agents before you hire any.

Chapter 18: Counting Down the Clock

Once you are certain that you want to invest in flipping a property, you will have a lot of things that you must accomplish along with certain questions that need answers. One of the most common questions investors have is: how long does it take to flip a house? Well, the time taken for flipping a property before the sale will vary from one property to another, so there is no fixed answer per se. However, there are certain numbers and deadlines you can keep in mind to calculate the time taken for a flipping project.

An optimistic estimation of the time taken to purchase a property can be anywhere between five to ten days. According to the method that you use to acquire the property, the time taken for it will vary greatly. You can use a Realtor, purchase a property at an auction, or make the decision based on self-conducted research. Apart from the research required to purchase the property, another aspect which influences this timeframe is the financing option you use. A hard money loan or paying upfront with cash is the quickest way to finalize a deal.

Flipping a property by renovating it can take anywhere between 45 days to three months. Having an organized crew with a reliable contractor is your safest bet. Any unplanned-for repairs like fixing structural damage, plumbing, roofing, or flooring issues can increase the time taken to flip a property.

Selling a property once it is flipped can take anywhere between 45 days and six months. According to how you want to sell the property, the time it takes can vary. An optimistic estimate is that you self-advertise the property for ten days, get some good leads, find a good buyer, and enter into an escrow with the potential buyer. This entire process can take anywhere between three to seven weeks. If the escrow closes on time like it is supposed to, then you will be able to sell your property within three months of purchasing it.

So, when you are estimating the time taken for flipping the property, it is a good idea to set the timeline such that it offers some flexibility.

Chapter 19: Where to Look to Find Flippable Properties

There are two steps involved while searching for properties you can flip. The first step is to select a specific market and then search for a property that meets your requirements.

Select a Market

So, you need to start by selecting a market. If you are just getting started with flipping, then the first place to look is your backyard. It means looking for a property within your own neighborhood. Having a market close to where you reside comes in handy since you can easily supervise the flipping work. Since it is your home turf, you will know the area well and will be aware of whether a place is popular or not. Being aware of these things helps when selling the property. You will also be aware of the present market trends and the value of the property. Flipping a property that is far away from your residence increases the time taken to travel and supervise the work and can also be a reason for added stress. Being close to the property also means that you have the option of showing the property to any interested buyers instead of always relying on a third party to do this work for you.

The home market you are looking at will also depend on the type of homes you want to flip. If you are just getting started with flipping, then you will want a property that offers the highest liquidity in the market like a single-family home. By opting for a property that offers high rates of sale and purchase means that there is sufficient demand and supply for such properties. Also, the equity required for flipping such properties will be significantly lower than flipping a high-end house.

While selecting the property, always look for ones who need moderate renovation work instead of any extensive projects. Until you have more experience with flipping houses, opting for extensive renovation work is not a good idea.

The next step is to start looking for the property after you are happy with your target market. The different ways to look for a property are through auctions, short sale, traditional means of MLS, through REO, and seller direct. The source you use to procure the property from can change according to the market conditions. For instance, when the prices are low, then an auction is a good place to look for properties while seller direct works well when the market is hot.

Auctions

The first option to consider if the market seems distressed is an auction. An auction can help you find underpriced properties that need to be renovated. Properties selling at an auction are usually foreclosed properties that are sold by the lender at a discount to minimize any losses in their balance sheets. The discount offered on auction properties offers arbitrage to investors, and the competition is usually low since such houses aren't listed on the general market. However, when you deal with a foreclosure auction, you must keep in mind that most of those properties tend to have certain liens on them, which you will inherit upon purchase. Ensure that the house you are acquiring at an auction has a clear title and that you have done the necessary research to understand the consequences of your decision thoroughly.

This is a great option, especially if you can pay for the property in cash or submit a cashier's check for it. Most of the lists for any foreclosed auctions to be held will be published a couple of weeks ahead. Also, private and estate auctions are also usually advertised about a few weeks in advance. By going through such listings, you can scope out the property in advance and see if you want to consider bidding on them.

Most of the auctioneers require the buyer to pay 10% of the purchase price down as soon as the sale is finalized, and you might have to pay for the rest within 30 days. So, ensure that your finances are in order and readily available if you want to enter an auction. Financing an auction purchase is tricky since it doesn't give lenders an option to conduct an appraisal or walkthrough of the property before the auction is closed.

REO

Another option available is to look for properties referred to as REO or real estate owned listings. Whenever a property doesn't get sold at an auction, the property will be owned by the lender or the bank and are known as REO. Since financial institutions don't deal in the business of buying or selling real estate, they are often too eager to liquidate such assets and might even be willing to sell the property at a reasonable discount. Along with any structural damage, you must watch out for any possible liens on the property before purchase.

Short Sale

A short sale takes place when the property owner defaults on any mortgage payment. The bank or the lender gives the property owner an okay to sell or "short" the property at a value that's lower than the debt owed as a mortgage. Banks tend to opt for a short sale instead of an auction since it saves them having to undergo the expensive and time-consuming process that is involved in auctioning a foreclosure property. If the short sale is approved by the bank, then it can be a good opportunity for the buyer to acquire the property at a discounted rate.

However, a short sale tends to take longer for completion than a conventional retail sale since the lender's approval is needed for the short sale and for deciding the sale price. Also, the lender might not agree to pay for any extras a usual seller agrees to, and this might mean higher closing costs for the property buyer. There are certain phrases you can look for in listing which imply that it is a short sale like "pre-foreclosure," "subject to the approval of the bank," "pre-approved by a bank," or "third-party review is necessary."

MLS

One of the conventional methods to find a listing for sale is through MLS or multiple-listing service. This service enables sellers to list their properties with various aggregators and websites across the Internet. It enables buyers to search through different listings posted by real estate agents and find a property. If a property is being sold, then it will most certainly be listed on MLS unless it is a foreclosed property or is being auctioned.

On the downside, the level of competition a buyer will face while searching for flippable properties on MLS is quite high. Since thousands of buyers can easily access the same information that you can, it will increase the competition, and the properties that are priced under the market rate will be snatched up quickly.

Seller Direct

When the property prices are high, and the market is doing well, finding properties to flip isn't easy. At times, some of the best deals available might not even be on the market yet since the seller hasn't decided. *Seller direct* or *direct-to-seller* refers to a means by which the interested buyer approaches the homeowners directly in a strategic fashion when their properties aren't listed yet, and makes an offer on the unlisted property.

There are certain tools like PropStream, Rebo Gateway, and FindMotivatedSellersNow, which collect and curate all the publicly available data and create a propensity to sell a model, and help predict when a certain homeowner might be interested in selling a property. Once you identify any such potential opportunity, you can then contact those potential sellers.

Groups and Forums

You can join a real estate investment forum, go to local meetups, and even join LinkedIn groups. These groups have become rather common in the last couple of years, and it might be a good idea to check the local groups in your area. These are great opportunities to learn from other investors and for networking. Apart from this, such groups often provide monthly newsletters with the available real estate listings. There are different online forums that you can access to search for buying properties like Biggerpockets.com, which offer all the information a real estate investor might need along the way.

Classifieds

Going through the listings in the classified section of the newspaper is another good idea. Looking through this section of the newspaper can provide you different properties listed for sale by the owner. The readership of newspapers has certainly reduced in the last couple of years, but it is still a good way to search for properties.

Wholesalers

You can also contact property wholesalers who buy and sell properties regularly. However, you must consider the markups they have on the property before you decide to purchase from a wholesaler. Wholesalers usually find rehab houses, put them under a contract, and then look for sellers who are interested in flipping the property. This might not be a cost-effective way to purchase a property for flipping, but it will certainly help save time and money later. With a quick Internet search or by going to real estate investment group meetings, you can meet property wholesalers.

Real Estate Agent

Besides all this, there is another way you can find properties for flipping - hire an agent. A real estate agent can help you find the ideal properties for flipping, and this is the reason why you need such a person on your property flipping team. A real estate agent can help you quickly filter through the different listings and help you find properties that meet your requirements. While looking for properties to flip, opting for an agent who specializes in real estate owned (REO) properties is a good idea. Most of the properties listed as REO tend to have undergone foreclosure, and maybe an eviction too. Apart from this, the previous occupants probably didn't take good care of the property wherein the mortgage has defaulted. As a result, these properties are often listed at a price lower than the market value.

Chapter 20: Apartments + Houses

While selecting a property for flipping, there are different options to choose from, including single-unit family homes, multiple-unit family homes, and condos.

Benefits of Multi-Dwelling Units

Here are the benefits a multi-dwelling unit offers over a single-unit family home.

The likely cash flow you can receive from a multi-unit property is more than the one from a single-unit property. If you ever plan to rent the flipped property, then the rent from multi-unit properties is greater than that of a single-unit home.

The market that multi-unit homes have is larger than the market for single-unit homes. The list of potential buyers for such properties includes investors as well as homeowners. Another advantage of investing in a multi-unit property is that it gives you the option of renting out some units while you are flipping the rest.

Multi-unit buildings offer economies of scale. If you are flipping several single-family homes, then there are different repairs you must undertake for each of those units. However, with a multi-unit dwelling building, you only have to worry about a single roof and a single heating system. Also, you don't have to keep traveling from one property to another since all the rehab work will be undertaken at one property.

The number of competitors present in the market for multi-unit dwellings is lower than the competition present for other types of properties. When the number of competitors is low, it helps create a level playing field.

Flipping a multi-unit building also offers certain tax advantages you can benefit from. By renting out a couple of units while you flip other portions for over a year can help deduct the profits from sales proceedings since it is a long-term capital gain. Also, the repair costs you incur can be excluded from the taxation requirements while renovating the property. If you decide to live on site, then you can also deduct the depreciation and expenses from that unit as a tax deduction.

Obstacles to Flipping Condos

Here are the different obstacles you might face while flipping condos.

While dealing with flipping condos, you will mostly have to deal with a homeowner's association. A lot of people shy away from investing in flipping condos because they don't like the idea of having to operate under the rules set by some other party. This does take away a little freedom from the investor. After all, one of the basic aspects of flipping that attracts investors is the fact that it gives the investor the freedom to flip the house as they want to, from the inside out.

You might run into buyers with a cookie-cutter mentality. A buyer with this mentality will not only value the property but will also expect it to be priced according to the value of other condos in the same building. Now, you might have spent a lot of your time, energy, and resources renovating the condo inside out and might have made expensive renovations to beautify the unit too. However, a cookie cutter buyer will expect the condo to be priced at the same rate as the other condos in the unit (the ones which haven't been flipped and come with only the bare necessities).

When you are flipping condos, you cannot make any external changes to the unit. All the work will be confined only to the interior rooms of the unit. You cannot install a new roof, work on landscaping, or even paint the exterior façade. With flipping houses, the curb appeal of the property goes a long way toward making a good first impression on the prospective buyer. You cannot leverage this benefit when flipping condos.

Chapter 21: Foreclosures

As mentioned earlier, foreclosure happens when the property owner defaults on their mortgage payments, and the lender or the bank repossesses the property. It certainly doesn't spell good news for a homeowner, but it is a good option if you are looking to flip properties. Flipping foreclosures is a sound investment decision, but there is a certain degree of unpredictability when it comes to these properties. Usually, foreclosed properties tend to be in worse condition than other real estate properties. Here are certain things you need to keep in mind when buying a foreclosed property.

The first thing is to purchase a foreclosed property at an auction. To do this, you must do all the homework: look for foreclosed properties and make a list of properties you might be interested in. You can contact mortgage companies, look for ads in the newspaper for any forthcoming listings, or even refer to the website of the U.S. Department of Housing and Urban Development.

You have to visit the property and see for yourself the condition the property is in. However, it isn't often that prospective buyers are allowed to access the insides of a foreclosed property. So, there is a certain degree of risk involved. It means you will not be able to get a total estimate of all the repair costs involved. The best way to go about doing this is by talking to the neighbors about the property in order to make a list of any potential damages you can anticipate. For instance, if you get to know from the neighbors that the previous owner had several pets, then you can anticipate some sort of animal damage.

Aside from viewing the property, you must redo your due

diligence on other comparable properties in the neighborhood that were recently sold. Doing this will help you gauge the likely market value of the property and the after repair value, and will ensure that you don't bid too high during the auction. Before the auction, you must decide the price limit for the property and bid accordingly. Don't let your emotions get in the way and bid according to your budget.

Since the recession in 2008, the foreclosure market has picked up quite a lot and has become a hot market for flippers.

Chapter 22: External Factors

The real estate market is influenced by different external factors that are beyond the investor's control. Regardless of whether you are interested in selling or buying a property, here are a couple of external factors that you must consider while making any real estate property investment decisions.

Economy

The economy is one of the most important external factors, and any unfavorable market conditions are usually the result of the condition of the economy. The national, state and local economies are interdependent, but they tend to vary from one region to another. The political climate, along with consumer confidence, tends to influence the economy and it is difficult to gauge their impact accurately. For instance, the Trump administration in the U.S. helped increase the employment rates, which in turn improved the economy's overall recovery. Factors like this can help people predict real estate trends in a specific area.

Natural Factors

Natural factors cannot be controlled, and they tend to have a massive impact on the real estate industry. For instance, hurricane Harvey that hit Houston managed to wreck a perfectly thriving real estate market within just four days. In the aftermath of the devastating storm, the real estate market wasn't in a good state. Not only properties were destroyed, but the listings also increased while the sale prices dropped steadily. After a year, the market started to return to its original form slowly, and this, in turn, increased the selling price, making it into a seller's market. The storm also brought about new housing trends like building a house at least ten feet above the ground level. Such trends meant house flipping became a growing trend. Investors were looking to fix and flip damaged properties and resell them.

Interest Rates

The interest rates are influenced by different factors like the global economy, politics, and banks. Any changes that take place in the international economies also tend to have an effect on the housing market in the U.S. However, interest rates are not left totally unregulated; the Federal Reserve does have a say in this matter. At times, any artificial control norms on the interest rates can spell trouble as it did during the 2008 housing bubble.

Demographics

Each generation has certain defining characteristics. For instance, until a couple of years ago, the millennial generation was partial toward renting properties instead of buying them. However, there has been a gradual shift in this trend, and it is moving toward homeownership. The changing demographic patterns tend to influence the way a real estate market function. Being aware of the cultural trends at the moment will help you understand the kind of properties that a specific group of demographics is looking for.

Porter's Five Forces

In 1979, Michael Porter, a professor at Harvard Business School, developed a tool that assists in analyzing the profitability and the appeal of an industry. This tool is referred to as Porter's Five Forces. Porter noticed that there are five factors that determine the profitability in an industry, and they are competing in the industry, the supplier power, buyer power, fear of substitution, and any new entrants.

The greater the competition in the market, the more difficult is it to make good profits. The number of suppliers in the market also influences the profit margin in an industry. The more suppliers are present, the easier it will be for you to switch to someone else. The more choice you have, the easier is to switch to a cheaper alternative and vice versa. The number of buyers in the market will determine the price. If the number of buyers is high in the market while the supply stays constant, then the prices will go up and vice versa. If there exists an option for substitution, wherein someone else can offer a cheaper substitute to what you offer, then the chances of your profit margin declining are quite high. Aside from all this, another factor that influences the profitability quotient of an industry is the ease of entry. The more selective and limited a niche is, the more profitable it is.

Chapter 23: The Laws

You might have found a property you want to invest in and might be looking forward to flipping the property. However, there are certain laws and regulations you must follow to ensure that you don't land up in any accidental legal trouble. In this section, you will learn about the different permits you need to ensure that you don't violate any laws while flipping properties.

There aren't any specific permits per se that you need while flipping houses, but having the right permits for the work you plan to do will save time along with money while flipping. Once you are certain of all the renovation work you want to undertake, it is time to make sure that the law provides for making such changes. Permits act as a guarantee that the worker is professional and insured and, in turn, can save the investor from unnecessary trouble. Also, a permit ensures that the property is safe to live in and the construction along with any repairs and renovations are in compliance with the local building code.

You can get a permit for the rehab work from the local municipality within which the property is located. If you hire a reputable contractor, the contractor will be the one who will obtain all the necessary permits before the work commences.

Here are some renovations that will definitely need a permit:

- To expand the square footage of the constructed portion of the property.
- To demolish a load-bearing wall.
- To install new wiring in the property.

- To install a fence that is over 6 feet high.

- To build a deck above a specific height.

- To make any changes that are related to a public sewer line.

Here are some changes for which you might need a permit:

- For any minor plumbing work involved, like shifting a sink.

- To demolish a non-load-bearing wall.

- To cut down any trees.

- To install a new window or door by cutting into the wall.

You don't need a permit for the following:
- To install a new roof.

- To include a dumpster within your property. Check with the local homeowner's association to ensure that this doesn't violate any of their rules.

- To install a new floor or change the flooring.

- To replace sinks.

- To repaint the house (although you cannot paint the external walls if you are flipping a condo).

- Replacing any of the existing doors and windows of the property.

- To install exterior siding.

- To replace any of the countertops.

- To do any minor electrical repairs like replacing an outlet, adding new lights, or changing the lighting.

- To build a deck within the permissible height.

- To build a wall within the permissible height.

Either talk to the contractor you hire or inquire with the local permitting office to ensure that you have all the necessary licenses before flipping a house.

Once the flipping job is complete, the party that issued the license will need to inspect the property. If the flipped property doesn't pass the inspection, then you will need to make the necessary changes to ensure that the property passes inspection. All of this can increase your costs and the work involved.

Ideally, as soon as you complete one portion of rehab work, you need to call the inspector to evaluate the work and sign off on it if the property meets all the requirements. If not, then you can make the necessary changes to ensure that you aren't violating any regulations.

For instance, if you had some wiring or plumbing jobs to be done, then ensure that you get an inspector to inspect the work done before installing the drywall. If the inspection is held after the drywall is installed, then it will need to be taken down for the inspector to examine the work completed. All this will increase your costs and time.

Make it a point to order inspections while the rehab work is going on. This will ensure that the contractor does a good job and keeps up the standard of work. Ensure that you pay the contractor whenever a job has been done satisfactorily. Include a clause stating this in the agreement you have with the contractor.

If the property passes one stage of inspection, you can move onto the next part of the rehab work being done. If the property fails an inspection, you will need to redo that work, and only then can you move onto the next portion.

Section 6: Viewing and Buying

Chapter 24: The Checklist

When you are viewing the properties you want to buy, there are certain things you must look out for. Let's discuss them here.

Exteriors

Notice the exteriors of the property before you decide to purchase. Look for any cracks or tilts, because repairing the exterior of a home can be expensive. While viewing the property, ensure that you bring a leveler along and ensure that any cracks aren't wider than 1/4 inch. Most sellers tend to cover any structural damage with some new paint. So, you must look for any surfaces or paint jobs that seem mismatched.

Ownership

You need to check the ownership history of the property. The way you might go through an individual's resume before hiring them, you will need to carefully go through the ownership history of the property and look for the average length of ownership for a property. If the turnover of the property is quite high, then it is a warning sign you cannot ignore.

Water Damage

Look out for any water damage that's been concealed with paint. When water damage isn't properly treated, and it is merely covered with paint, it leads to the accumulation of moisture in the walls and can also cause mold. If this mold turns out to be black mold, then it is toxic to breathe. You need to examine the underside of the kitchen sinks, drawers, and the tubs or toilets in the house. If you notice any sheetrock under the window seals, it means there are leaks in the property.

Uneven Flooring

Checking for uneven floors can help save you from making an expensive mistake. Bouncy or uneven flooring cannot be fixed easily, and the older the house is the more carefully must you scrutinize the flooring. A simple way to test whether the flooring is even or not is a simple marble test. You just need to place the marble on the floor in different floors. If the marble tilts in one direction and rolls away, then the flooring isn't even.

Excessive Room Fresheners

Beware of the use of any excessive air fresheners. Room fresheners are often used to cover up any stink like sewage, leaky pipes, or even mold.

Music to Cover Noise

If there is music playing in every room, then it is usually done to mask any noises from outside. So, make it a point to insist that the music, along with the air conditioners, are all turned off while viewing a property to check whether the noise levels are tolerable or not.

Other Red Flags

If a seller prevents you from checking any areas like a crawlspace or a room, then it is a red flag you cannot afford to ignore. If a seller is doing this, it is probably because the seller has something to hide.
If a seller is offering any incentives to waive off a specific inspection, then it means the property might not pass such an inspection. Always inspect the property and never agree to waive any inspections.
You must always ask for the Report of Residential Building Record (or 3R report) while viewing a property. This report lets you understand whether any repairs or work done to the property are in accordance with the local rules and laws or not. The 3R report is like a report card for the property. If a new deck was installed, then it must be included in the 3R report. If it isn't mentioned in the report, then such a deck might violate certain codes and might be unsafe too.

Inspect the Property

If the hedge is unkempt and the property also looks like it is poorly maintained, then be super vigilant while inspecting. Whenever you visit a property you might want to buy, you have to be vigilant. You need to inspect the foundation, check the electrical box, check the alignment of the floor, and inspect anything at all that looks even slightly suspicious to you.

Chapter 25: Do the Numbers Add Up?

Stay practical and realistic when selecting a property. Don't make the mistake of buying property just because it appeals to you. You must ensure that your finances line up with all the reasonable expenses you might face. When you are calculating the budget for flipping a property, there are certain key factors you have to take into consideration.

Rehab and Renovation Works

The first cost is related to all the rehab and renovation work you plan to undertake. Flipping a property by making changes to its structure will be more expensive than making simple cosmetic repairs. Cosmetics repairs, like changing the cabinets, changing the basic electrical fixtures, replacing any damaged sockets, or giving a fresh coat of paint to the interior walls, can greatly improve the appearance of the property. By reducing the costs of renovation, you can improve your ROI. Certain repairs like renovating the kitchen, bathrooms, or painting the façade are considered to be moderate repairs. You need a licensed contractor who can undertake all these repairs and satisfactorily do them. Aside from this, you must also consider the time it will take to make all these repairs. The longer you take to flip the house, the costlier the flipping process will be. This is because the carrying costs tend to increase, like the financing, property taxes due, and the utility bills.

Taxes and Fees

There are different taxes, legal, and insurance costs involved while renovating a property. It is essential that you purchase property insurance while flipping. Property insurance tends to differ from one place to another. So it is important that you are aware of the average costs in your area and include that in your budget too. Contractors will need certain utilities like water, electricity, and lights to keep working. So, while the renovation work is underway, you will be required to pay for all these utilities too. To get an idea of the likely costs involved, talk to the previous owner of the property and ask them about their utility bills. You must also consider all the amounts payable to your flipping team.

Marketing Costs

Apart from this, you need to account for marketing costs too. Flipping a property will not do you any good until you sell it. There are different marketing techniques you will need to employ to get the ball rolling, and these things cost money. You need more than a "for sale" sign and word of mouth to sell a property. The best way to go about doing this is by hiring a Realtor to help sell the property. You need to remember to include the fee of the Realtor while calculating the marketing expenses.

Calculate ARV

Once you are aware of all the potential costs you can incur, you need to start crunching numbers yet again.

You must calculate your ARV or after-repair value to help determine the budget for flipping a property. ARV refers to the final value of the property after all the renovation and rehab work is completed.

You can determine the ARV by comparing the selling price of similar properties within the neighborhood in the past three months. You can calculate ARV by using a simple formula.

ARV = Total purchase price of the property + Cost of all repairs

Once you determine the ARV, you must determine the best bidding price for the property. The general rule of thumb is to go with 70% of ARV. So, the formula to determine the best purchase price for the house is 70% of ARV minus all the repair works. For instance, if the property you like has an ARV of $150,000 and it needs about $40,000 as repairs, then the best price you can pay for the property is $65,000. Also, include a little rolling cash to be kept as a buffer for any unforeseen expenses.

Calculate ROI

The next thing you must do is calculate the ROI. The return on investment will help determine whether flipping the property will be profitable or not. You can calculate the ROI in two ways: the out-of-pocket method and the cost method.

In the out-of-pocket method, you will be considering all the money that you spend out of your pocket for flipping a property. If you are financing the property, along with any down payment and renovation costs, then you must use this method.

For instance, let us assume that you spend $15,000 for the down payment the property and estimate that the repairs will amount to $30,000. Then the out of pocket expense you incur is $45,000. After you make all the renovations, the property is valued at $180,000, then the equity you have will be $135,000 ($180,000 - $45,000). By dividing this equity by the total value of the property, you will get an ROI of 75%. It might seem like a good deal on paper, but please remember that the percentage projected is high because you are paying cash up front. This method considers all the out of pocket expenses while leveraging the finances to yield a high ROI.

You can calculate the ROI by considering all the costs that you incur and then dividing the equity you have in the property by the total costs. For instance, if you are purchasing a rental property for $130,000 and then spend $12,000 on repairs. This means your total investment in the property is $142,000. If the monthly rent of the property is $1100, then you will earn $13,200 as rent per year. Now, you must account for property taxes and insurance too. Let us assume that you pay $200 per month toward these two expenses, and the total amount payable is $2,400 per year. So, here is how you will be calculating the ROI.

The net operating income you will receive is the rental income you earn after deducting any expenses. In this case, it will be $10,800 per year ($13,200 - $2,400). Now, to calculate the ROI, you must divide your net income by the total investment you make. So, ROI is $10,800/ $142,000 = 7.6%.

Chapter 26: How to Get Capital

Now that you know you are ready to get started with flipping properties, it is essential that you learn about your financing options. Here are certain ways in which you can raise the necessary capital.

HELOC

You can get a home equity line of credit (HELOC). It is quite similar to using a credit card instead of a conventional loan. The bank will grant you a credit line based on the value of your home or property. Instead of withdrawing everything at once, you can start drawing out small amounts as and when the need arises. For instance, if you need $1,000 to refurbish and remodel the kitchen, then you can take that amount first and then move onto the next portion of flipping. Also, you are required to pay interest only for the amounts you withdraw. This is a very good option, especially if the renovation work is going to be a slow one.

Bank Financing

Although many house flippers are skeptical of using conventional bank financing, this may also be an option. A lot of flippers don't opt for this option because the interest payable on such loans tends to be quite high, and there might even be certain penalties for any defaults in payments. Conventional means of finance also rely on your credit score along with the debt ratio. Even if the loan you are taking is not a personal one, most lenders tend to hesitate to give a loan to someone who has a mortgage already. If you can qualify for a loan and are more comfortable with conventional financing, then opting for this is a good idea. However, consult your accountant or a banker while deciding the source of finance.

Hard Money Loan

A hard money loan is designed for those who don't have a good credit score or might want to repay the loan within a short period like a year or two. It has become rather easy to qualify for such loans these days, and you will receive the loan amount within two weeks. If you are certain that you can turn in a quick profit, then opting for a hard money loan can be ideal. However, the interest rates chargeable on such loans are quite high and start at 7% or more. You will also need to repay the loan within the agreed-upon period regardless of whether you have sold the property or not.

Investors

You can seek personal investors for your flipping project. You can opt for peer-to-peer lending by seeking loans from your personal circle. You can also solicit multiple investors for the financing you require. You can either agree to pay them a portion of the profits you make or pay a certain interest on the loan when it is given out. If you are looking for investors, then it always helps to have a couple of successful flips in your pocket so that you can earn their confidence.

Cash-Out Refinance

You can opt for a cash-out refinance if you own any other real estate properties at present. In this method, you will be essentially refinancing an existing property to raise the capital for the new investment. You can take a loan for a value that's slightly over the value of your existing property. The loan that you take on can be used to repay an existing mortgage, and according to the equity you have in the existing property; you can use it to finance your other project. You will essentially be receiving the difference in the amount of the new loan and the previous mortgage. The interest rates on refinancing options are low when compared to a traditional mortgage. But to use this option, you must not only own property, but you also have to already have significant equity.

Crowdfunding

Real estate crowdfunding has become quite popular these days. You can use this option to collect the financing you need. You will essentially be gathering a series of small or large investments and redirecting them toward a new project. Investors in crowdfunding will either receive interest or get a share in the profits. This is considered to be slightly tricky and risky because it is a new practice and doesn't show much consistency. However, this is one option you can explore if all else fails.

401k

If you have an employer 401k plan and are contributing to it, then you can take out a loan against the principal in your 401k. You can draw a loan of about $50,000 or 50% of your holding, whichever is less. This can be quite helpful since you will not be repaying the amount to a third-party. Instead, all the repayments you make will be deposited in your account itself. However, this is considered to be very risky because if the flip doesn't go as intended, you stand to lose your savings.

Chapter 27: Closing the Deal

In this section, you will learn about the different techniques you can use to negotiate and successfully close a deal.

When to Stop

It is often said that the best negotiation strategy is to prepare yourself to leave the table if a deal is not suitable for you. An even more important strategy is to determine which deals don't suit you. Just explain that your bottom line is not enough. Instead, write down your bottom line and notify your friends and family about the same. So, you will be ashamed if you succumb to the emotions of the negotiations and deviate from their nature. Indeed, the emotions of closing a deal are often insurmountable, but making a bad deal is far less beneficial than avoiding a bad deal and saving your money for a better investment.

The Narrative

The narrative you come up with must be a combination of solid mathematics and good storytelling. In terms of mathematics, the negotiator can justify his position.

Numbers

When it comes to math, a good negotiator will be able to justify their positioning with substantive evidence. Before choosing a position, a good real estate negotiator will have a comparative analysis of similar properties that were traded in the market at the same time in the previous year. If you want to negotiate a deal successfully, then you must not only focus on numbers but also ensure that the narrative you come up with is compelling. A good narrative can help lower the costs if done tactfully.

Avoid Bias

A good negotiator also knows how to avoid illegal, discriminatory issues that may violate federal, state, and local laws on fair housing and human rights. The different issues you must steer clear of while negotiating are race, ethnicity, religion, color, national origin, immigration status, citizenship status, sexual orientation, legal income, marital status, partnership status, military status, gender, gender identity, age, disability, victims of domestic violence, victims of sexual violence, and victims of persecution. The discussion of these protected classes is not only prohibited, but may also result in a significant financial risk of liability for consequential punitive damages and attorney's fees in the future discrimination lawsuit.

You must work on positional bargaining. For instance, if you offer $100,000 on a listing of $150,000 and the seller makes a counteroffer of $125,000, this process can go on for a while where both the parties come up with numbers they think are fair until they can reach an agreement.

External Factors

Often the position of a party is based on an external influence, and if that influence is not known and understood, negotiations are not effective. The seller may be motivated to sell because he has a sick relative abroad, a chance to work, a new child, or some other factor. Without knowing this factor, the buyer simply throws money at the business if the money does not solve the invisible motivator. In the picture, faster closing may be more valuable to the seller than more money.

When you negotiate the terms of a sale or lease through a real estate agent, this is like playing a game of phone tag. Yes, estate agents have a fiduciary duty to notify and inform, but most negotiations are about not what is said but what hasn't been said: the non-verbal signals. Therefore, it is extremely important to ask, line by line, what the real estate agent has experienced during the negotiations. Understanding the nuances of the negotiations will inform you of the final decision and the reasons for that decision. Ask your real estate agent exactly what was said, how the words were expressed when everything was said during negotiations. Only by listening to the other side, not just hearing what they said, can you create a true negotiating strategy for the next strategic step.

Communications

Contract memoranda, transaction sheets, sales notes, and sales agreements are documents that can constitute a binding contract if no action is taken. Always ask your broker to include the following clause in the messages created on your behalf: "*** This correspondence is for negotiation only ***, _____ [Realtor name] is not authorized to give final information or execute agreement on behalf of our customer. The execution of a separate formal contract is a necessary condition of a contract of sale (or lease), and without it, there is no definitive binding agreement. There are other essential conditions besides those proposed here, and our customer will not agree to any purchase agreement (or lease) without these essential terms." Do not sign any of the above agreements until the agreement has been fully reviewed by your lawyer, and you receive a complete picture of your costs and benefits from the transaction. You cannot force anyone to conclude an agreement that they have not yet completed. Until the formal agreement is broken and crossed, you have nothing. As they say, do not count your chickens until they hatch. Look at the price until you have a full contract.

Formalizing the Agreement

The final step is to formalize the agreement. There are four elements that must be present for the agreement to be formalized. There needs to be an offer, certain conditions, the acceptance of the offer, and the consideration for that offer's acceptance. If any of these elements are missing from the contract, then it becomes voidable. Even the presence of fraudulent terms or inclusion of any illegal consideration can also result in the contract becoming voidable. Remember that you need to make it a point to stay calm and patient during the negotiation proceedings.

FBI Negotiating Tactics

The behavioral change stairway model was created by the hostage negotiation unit of the FBI for negotiating a high stakes situation. Well, this technique can be used for not just hostage negotiation, but any other form of negotiation, including real estate negotiations. There are five simple steps included in this model, and they are active listening, empathy, rapport, influence, and behavioral change.

You must start listening actively to what the other party says, and you must make them feel like you are listening to them. You must understand where they are coming from and the reasons for the way they feel. Empathy is a great way to establish rapport with someone. Once you show empathy, a rapport will be established, and you can earn the other person's trust. Once you earn their trust, it becomes easier to influence them. You can start offering different solutions to reach a mutually beneficial conclusion. Once all this is done, the other party will act in a positive manner, and the negotiation can come to an end.

Even if you feel like you are going through all these steps, it is likely that you are mostly following only the last two steps. Most of us tend to jump directly to the fourth step of trying to influence the other person to act in a manner that's favorable to us. Don't go with the "this is why what I am saying is right and you are wrong" approach since it will do you no good. Instead of all this, appealing to the other person's logic is the best way to get a favorable response. So, how can you apply these tactics while negotiating a real estate deal?

The first thing you need to do is prove your listening skills. To do this, you must ask the buyer or the buyer's real estate agent certain open-ended questions that cannot be answered with a single word like yes or no. If you are trying to sell the property or you are buying a property, try to create a rapport. For instance, if you want to sell a single-family unit home that you flipped and are showing the property to a couple. If you are aware of the fact that the couple is planning a family, then while showing the property, you can suggest that the bedroom next to the master bedroom can be decorated as a nursery. If you know that the potential buyer is involved in the music industry, then ensure that you play some soothing and relaxing music in the background to show off the new sound system you included in the house. If you know that the buyer is looking to make a home library, then set up a coffee table book that is strategically opened to a page that shows pictures of beautiful home libraries when showing the property. Regardless of whether you are trying to buy or sell a property, you must appeal to the other person's human side and not just treat it like a routine business deal. Never underestimate the value of emotions when it comes to negotiation.

Section 7: Let's Make Some Money

Chapter 28: Increasing the Value

The relationship with your contractor have a direct impact on your investment business. There are way too many terrible stories and instances of investors who worked with unprofessional contractors or contractors unfit for the job. There are small things you can do that make a big difference, and one of those things is to determine whether the contractor you hire will be good for your business or not. You must be sure that you hire the right contractor because the majority of the flipping work will be done by them. Of course, you want to make sure that you hire the right contractor, but you also want to go about doing it in the right way. If you maintain good relationships with your contractor, you never know how this could pay off in the future.

Even if you pay the contractor for the work, you should take some time to make his work less complicated and easier to understand. Think of the contractor as your ally instead of thinking about them as a person you have hired to do your work. If you want to increase the value of what you receive from this relationship, then you must treat your contractor as a partner and maintain a good long-term relationship. You never know when you might need a contractor in the future, and it certainly helps to have someone reliable to call in case of any emergencies.

This means creating a pleasant and clean working

environment. Some of the biggest confusions and disagreements between investors and contractors arise from the fact that they do not have a shared vision and are not on the same page about the work that has to be done. First, you must specify what your goals are, what your budget is, and in what time frame you want everything to be completed. It sounds simple enough, but the more you can get out of the way before the first tool is removed, the smoother the process becomes.

It is a good idea to complete all the non-contractor-related work beforehand. Most investors tend to be lazy and seem to think that their contractor can do and will take care of everything. Even if that's the case, that does not mean that they will necessarily want to do that. If you have any demo work, then ensure that you get someone to clean up the space before you get there.

If there will be several people working on the property at any given time, then it is a good idea to ask the contractor what their priority is and have the people work alongside the contractor. However, this doesn't mean you are not free to express your opinions. It simply means that you are extending basic courtesy toward someone to establish a good working relationship.

Once the work has started, you should do your best not to interfere. No contractor likes micro-management or likes being told how to do their job. If you trust your contractor enough to hire them, you should step back and let them work. You have the full right to visit your projects at your discretion, but you do not have to criticize every area of everything that is done. Take the time to get started, and check the timeframe for payments and the rest of your work schedule. The more you can go out of your way before you start, the smoother it will all be.

Ensure that you make the rules of payment - along with the payment time and amount - clear to the contractor from the beginning. This is the cause of most disagreements between contractors and investors. If you have to let your contractor wait until the very end to get paid, do you think they will want to work with you again? The best idea is to create a payment plan when the work is done. It may be the first Friday after completion or a fixed date contingent upon the completion of some given task. You have to be timely and punctual with your payments. By doing this simple thing, you can improve the relationship you have with the contractor.

There are also small things you can do to stand out from the crowd of investors. If you know you will visit the site in the morning, take coffee and breakfast for everyone who is at work. When you come in the afternoon, you can take some sandwiches over or offer to pay for lunch. You do not need to do these things, and some argue that you are reducing their effectiveness by doing them, but it can be argued that this will ensure that your contractor is satisfied and wants to do more work for you. A loyal and productive contractor can help you grow your investment business.

Chapter 29: What to Fix?

The revaluation of investment property is usually a sensible strategy if properly executed. Successful proponents of the "correct and throw" philosophy are investors with the motto "buy cheap, sell high." Therefore, they buy worn-out homes at competitive prices and save money on repairs, doing most of the work themselves. A little sweat capital is important to make real estate investments profitable. They also carefully choose their renovation projects, focusing on those that maximize returns at the lowest cost. Part of the process is to look at other houses in the neighborhood to avoid over-improving the properties. If none of the other houses in the area have crowns and tabletops, these amenities are unlikely to result in a significantly higher retail price.

Owners, on the other hand, often take a less strategic approach to rebuilding their homes. This can result in them investing significantly more money in the project than they return after the sale. While it is reasonable to make some improvements, do not overdo it.

How do you know which updates are worth the effort and which are not? To get the most out of your remodeling, remember four types of projects: basics, deterrence, value creation, and personal preferences.

The most important things that buyers expect when buying a home include a roof that does not leak, well-functioning gutters and downspouts, a dry basement, a sturdy stove, solid floors, walls in good condition and functioning retaining walls. Most potential buyers also expect plumbing, air conditioning, ventilation, and heating systems to function properly.

This does not mean that you should update it all. Instead, you can focus on regular maintenance and smaller, cheaper improvements that will assure proper operation.

Adding these items to a house where they are not present will not add value. It simply brings the property up to the standard level of the remaining houses in the neighborhood and allows you to charge a competitive price.

Also, you must ensure that your property stands out from all the competitors' properties. You must not make any unreasonable improvements that are extravagant as compared to other properties in the region. Not only will you lose money, but it will also scare off potential buyers too. In short, before you invest a lot of money in a complex full-house renovation project, you should consider what competing for real estate in your area could offer. Find out how similar properties in your area are valued and improve them according to your specific market.

Items that increase the curb appeal make the property look good when potential buyers arrive. Although these projects may not bring any significant monetary value to the property itself, they will help sell the place faster. Attractive features include a well-kept lawn, low-cost landscaping, fresh interior and exterior paint (at least the front door), clean carpets and new facilities (even tinkering with address numbers). You can do these projects yourself and save two important resources - time and money.

If you are trying to make the property look more attractive, then now is not the time for any bold changes to the scenery. Instead, try to come up with quick fixes that will instantly improve the appeal of the house. Something as simple as adding a sheer accent wall or even chic back panels with simple designs can improve the way the house looks. Another element that you can change without burning a hole in your pocket is lighting. By changing the lights and opting for soothing and pleasant LED lamps and lights, you can make the house look bright and fresh. If you need any help with these home improvement projects, then you can always contact an interior designer. Just make sure that you don't go overboard with these expenses and stick to a predetermined budget. Quick fixes like changing the lighting and the lighting fixtures in the house not only make the house look attractive, but are cost effective too.

Projects that offer significant added value are big favorites for all those who fix and flip properties, and they should also be high on the list of homeowners. Although most of these efforts will not pay back, some will come close. New siding, kitchen refurbishment (new countertops and the latest technology) and new windows are considered to be the most profitable projects, since they improve the appeal of the property and increase its resale cost. Other home improvement repairs you can opt for are upgrading the fixtures in the bathroom, renovating the patio, and adding energy-saving equipment to the house like solar water heaters also help improve the property's appeal.

There might be certain projects you might want to work on while flipping a property, but please keep in mind that your target audience might not want to pay for such changes. Personal preference projects include installing swimming pools, adding wine cellars, creating artificial ponds, or even adding fountains to the property. These are things that you might want to add to the property because they appeal to you. However, it is not a guarantee that your target buyer will feel the same way. Not only are such additions expensive, but also they might not really increase the property's value.

Second, many home buyers see a swimming pool as a problem that requires high operating costs and security - and something that can be used only a few months a year unless you live in a tropical climate.

There's nothing wrong with adding these items to your home, of course, but do not expect potential buyers to pay a premium to get them when you are ready to sell. And be careful when updating means replacing a popular or regular feature. If there is a two-car garage in another house near you, you should probably not be considering turning your home into a playroom. Do you want to be the only home in the area without secure parking?

Other tricky transformations include:

- The transformation of the bedroom into a studio.

- Removal of walls to increase the space (for instance, to create a flow between the dining room and the kitchen).

- Removing a bedroom to expand space.

- Upgrading the basement (small improvements, such as increasing storage capacity, will cost much more than a full upgrade or upgrade).

Chapter 30: DIY vs. Contracting

Paying the money up front when purchasing a property is the first step. You will also need to pay for different expenses that will crop up along the way like property tax, repairs, utility bills, and insurance. As a property owner, you might have to spend anywhere between 1 to 2% of your total property value on repairs every year. This figure only includes certain routine maintenance expenses, and if you are planning for renovation or remodeling work, then the costs involved will definitely increase.

For most remodeling jobs, the major expense you must pay for is labor. In fact, for most of the jobs, the cost of the labor is greater than the actual repairs made. For instance, to realign a door, it costs about $5 for the necessary supplies. However, you will need to pay the handyman anywhere between $30 to $130 per hour of work and a minimum payable fee of $150 to $300.

In some cases, you can avoid all these costs by doing the repairing or remodeling work by yourself. However, this doesn't mean that you must do all the repair and remodeling work yourself just because you might be able to do it. There are certain complicated tasks like electrical work, tile resetting, and plumbing projects that are best left to the professionals. On the other hand, there are certain jobs like a basic painting which you can do on your own with little or even no experience.

The question is: how do you decide which jobs you can do by yourself and when you need professional help? There are three factors that you must consider while deciding if you can opt for a DIY approach or need to hire a contractor. The three factors are as follows:

Safety Matters

The first factor you have to consider is whether the project is safe for you to undertake or not. There are three things you need to look out for while deciding whether a DIY job is dangerous or not. The first question is: what is the worst outcome of the DIY repair work you want to do? For some repairs, like fixing the roof or doing any major electrical work, the worst that can happen is you can be fatally wounded. You can never opt for DIYing those jobs that can compromise your safety or put you in harm's way. The next question you must ask yourself is whether the job you want to do can harm the property or not. If you are thinking about doing any major plumbing jobs, then the worst outcome of such a job is that it can cause severe damage to the property. For instance, removing and reinstalling bathroom fixtures can be included in this category. If the job isn't well done, then it can cause some small leaks that go unnoticed for a while. If such a leak isn't fixed in time, it can cause structural damage. Of course, hiring a plumber will save you all this grief. If a specific job requires a permit, then you absolutely cannot attempt to do it yourself. Any repair or renovation work that requires a permit stating that the job is done is a safe manner and guarantees the safety of the property are best left to the professionals.

Necessary Knowledge and Skills

The next factor you have to take into consideration is whether or not you have the necessary knowledge to undertake a specific job. You must know how to do the job, or else you cannot opt for taking the DIY approach. Having no experience whatsoever in fixing a leaky toilet or a door hinge is fine, you can learn about it easily and get the job done. However, there are certain complicated tasks like pouring concrete or even moving any plumbing fixtures that require technical know-how. Please avoid doing these jobs by yourself. Here are a couple of reasons why you have to seek professional help while tackling such difficult jobs. The first reason is that it can prove to be dangerous, and not taking the necessary care can be a health risk. Also, it is possible that any mistakes you make while trying to do the necessary repairs could prove to be costly ones. It is better to pay extra and hire a contractor to do the job correctly instead of doing it yourself and making the problem worse.

Time Taken

Another thing you must consider while deciding between DIY repairs and hiring a contractor is the time it will take. When it comes to investing, time is money. The first thing you have to do is calculate the costs of hiring a professional and the costs of doing it yourself. Once you figure out both these costs, the next step is to determine the time it will take to complete the job. For instance, consider a scenario where a DIY job takes about three weeks and costs $1,500, but the same job can be completed within a week and costs $2,000 if you hire a contractor. Well, in such a case, it is a good idea to seek professional help. Even if you do end up spending a little more money, you can rest easy knowing that the work done will be of good quality and you will save time, to boot.

Chapter 31: Negotiating with Contractors

It's hard to say if you've got a good deal on a home improvement project when you have nothing to compare it to. For this reason, it is always useful to have at least three comparable proposals or estimates for a project.

Most contractors will readily agree to certain contract terms when competing for work. However, it is your duty to provide the contractor with as many details about the project as you possibly can. You must also carefully go through any reviews of the contractors and compare them before deciding to hire any of them. It is always helpful to review the experience and expertise of the contractor before making a hiring decision. If you are okay with hiring a contractor with less experience, then you might be able to reduce the fees you'll have to pay.

You can also position yourself better in the negotiations by examining the costs of the materials to be used in the project. If you have a list of material costs, you can determine if the contractor is charging you a fair price for all the supplies required for the project.

Usually, a lot of contractors will offer to procure the materials required for the project and give their estimates to you later along with the invoices. Well, if this is the case, then be sure that you carefully check the prices of the items mentioned to ensure that the contractor is purchasing it for the best price and isn't skimming profits for himself.

To reduce your expenses, you can start buying the consumables yourself to make the best proposal for materials needed for the project. However, check the required quantity again with your contractor and make sure that you have enough material to complete the work in order to avoid delays in the project.

With the volume of resale growing, buyers are looking for ways to save money by buying consumables themselves, without necessarily weighing the pros and cons.

In general, the cost of your home improvement project depends in part on the season in which the project is carried out. You may be able to save money by looking for estimates at a time when construction is generally slower, and contractors are more willing to negotiate the costs.

If you live in a colder climate and want to add a room, for example, you should call the contractors to get estimates in the winter. Although work may start during higher temperature weather, you can negotiate lower costs while work is slow for the contractor.

When talking about your contract value, always keep your cards close to your chest. You may not want the contractor to know your entire situation, as certain details may contribute to his willingness to negotiate a price. Just give details of the work you want to have done and let the contractor speak.

If you and the contractor are satisfied with the prospect, you can offer to pay subcontractors or get the delivery of materials made directly to the site, instead of having to route it through the contractor. Doing this can help you save money spent as contractor's charges and it doesn't require any extra paperwork for you to worry about. You can also try to negotiate a better deal with the subcontractor for lowering the charges or even with the suppliers to reduce the cost of supplies.

If you and the contractor don't agree on the price and are at loggerheads about some expenses, it will certainly affect the quality of the work being done. To avoid all this and establish a good working relationship, it is a good idea to include the terms of payment in the work agreement that you sign before getting started with the fix and flip work. You must think of the contractor as your biggest ally when it comes to flipping houses.

If the contractor has some suggestions to revamp the property at a lower cost, then make sure you hear them out and take those suggestions into consideration.

Chapter 32: Outside Revamp

Here are a couple of things you can do to revamp the façade of the property and make it more appealing. Cut the bushes. Simple pruning of overgrown shrubs can greatly enhance the attractiveness of the home. Sometimes getting rid of certain bushes when they start to look too wild can instantly beautify the property.

If you have a house over which a tree hangs, you can cut those branches or even take down the whole tree if it makes the property look less appealing. The other advantage is that you also add light to the inside when you take down over an overhanging tree. This gives you a dual advantage. Often, improving the interior is just as if not more dramatic than improving the curb appeal. If you feel like the house must be repainted, then don't hesitate to get it done. However, you usually don't have to do this, even if it on first glance it seems that way. Closely inspect the condition of the walls before you decide to repaint it. If there is any mildew, you need to treat it first before repainting. Instead of opting to repaint the walls, you can also opt for a whitewash. When all this is done, the appearance of the house is greatly improved.

Adding new bushes along with flowerbeds can improve the curb appeal and gives the house a touch of color. Several new shrubs and some flowering plants can be added to not only make the house seem more decorative, but it also helps cover any parts of the property that aren't attractive like an ugly foundation. Whether you do this depends largely on the season and your location.

Another simple way in which you can improve the curb appeal is by weeding out the garden or the lawn. By getting rid of weeds, you can ensure that only the desirable plants grow. Also, weeds can ruin the aesthetics of a property and suffocate the growth of other plants you want there.

By simply mowing the lawn and watering it regularly, you can make it look healthy, vibrant, and attractive. A good-looking lawn improves the overall curb appeal of a property. Ensure that you weed and fertilize the lawn regularly. The lawn must not have any bare spots on it and if there are exposed areas then you need to fill them with new patches of grass.

A good and well-maintained driveway can create a stunning first impression. You can easily do this without burning a hole in your pocket. You must get the driveway refilled every three to ten years, and the frequency of this maintenance work primarily depends on the weather. If you plan to do it yourself, then it will cost you less than $100.

By installing a new mailbox, you can also improve the curb appeal. A rustic mailbox looks quite welcoming and lends a quaint look to the façade of the property. You can install a mailbox for $100 or less, including the installation charges and the raw materials.

If you notice that the front door doesn't look to be in good condition, then you will want to change it out. Apart from all this, you can lay down a walkway from the curb to the front door. A stone walkway looks appealing and can add symmetry to the property.

Section 8: Get Ready to Sell

Chapter 33: How to Sell

There are a couple of different things that you must keep in mind when you think about selling the property. Including good photos along with good descriptions can make the difference between getting a good deal on a property and the property being left unsold.

The Right Time

You have to make sure that you are selling the property at the right time. Real estate tends to be seasonal, and if you want to sell the flipped property quickly, then be sure that you are doing it at the right time. For instance, the ideal time to list a property for sale is between March and May since most property deals tend to be finalized during this time. The sales of properties tend to increase at the beginning of a new financial year instead of during or at the end of a financial year.

Pricing

You must ensure that the property you want to sell is priced properly. If you price the property too high, you might not get any buyers, and if it is too low, then you will end up short selling. So, it is essential that you assess the value of the flipped property from the beginning. By doing this, you can ensure that you are selling it at the right price and aren't wasting any time figuring out the sale price when the time for the sale is already upon you. You can assess similar properties in your area and decide the price at which you want to sell. For instance, if you notice that a house across the street from yours is being sold for a certain amount, ask yourself if you would be willing to pay the full amount to acquire that property, or will you want to consider reducing the price? Do this simple exercise to understand whether the property is priced correctly.

Online Profile

Most shoppers search the Internet for a new home, where pictures are king. When it comes to selling a home quickly, you should not publish too few or any unattractive photos or pictures with poor quality - this distracts potential buyers and may turn them away. The images should be of high quality and taken with a 5-megapixel camera or better, and not with a mobile phone. The photos must appeal to the buyer and must prompt them to take an interest in your property. However, be sure that you don't make the photos seem too staged or fake. The photos you take must be well lit and must show the property from different angles that show both the interiors and exteriors.

Right Description

The right words are just as important when it comes to selling your home. Share with potential buyers how impressive your home and the neighborhood are, including information on nearby schools, shopping, or regular activities offered near your home. Include information that showcases certain other fetching details about the property and the surrounding areas along with the basic information. The buyer needs to feel like they are looking at a special property.

You have to make sure that the house looks good, is in good condition, and has the features and amenities that will appeal to your target buyers.

Chapter 34: No One Buying?

The price is one of the most important determinants of the sale of real estate. If the price is too high, you can end up spending much more time on the market than you would like. By researching and comparing other properties, you can see if your offer matches the rest of the market. However, compare similar properties in the environment to achieve a realistic price range.

It can only take a few seconds for the buyer's attention to be drawn, especially when searching online. The more attractive your ads are, the better. If you think the current promotional materials for your home are boring and tired, talk to your real estate agent about how to take new photos and create new ads. You can also advertise on various media to reach a wider audience.

If you find that several people are visiting home showings but are not receiving offers, the presentation could be a problem. Real estate must have the best possible presentation in order to attract buyers. This means minimizing confusion and personal items, keeping the rooms clean, tidy, and spacious.

You can make some cost-effective improvements that do not take much time and improve the performance of the object. Especially for the first impression of the property, a fresh coat of paint or the tidying up of the back yard can play a decisive role.

Depending on the current real estate market, you may find that you have entered the market at the wrong time. The longer a property is listed on the market, the fewer the chances that a buyer will opt for it. If the market seems unfavorable at the moment, you can relist the property after a couple of weeks or months when the market is back in full swing. This is where the virtue of patience will come in handy.

At this point, consider taking real estate off the market and return it in a few months. During this time, new buyers will be looking for real estate, and you will have an expanded audience for sale.

Seeing how other houses in the market work can improve your marketing strategy. Visit open houses and auctions of other properties in your area to get an idea of how they are presented and at what price they are sold. You may find that selling at an auction or privately in your area can be more successful.

When selling real estate, it is important not to consider your personal opinions when making a decision. Professionals, such as estate agents and other industry experts, can provide objective and honest feedback on why your property is not selling.

Chapter 35: Close the Deal

The process of closing houses for sellers begins as soon as offers are received. Prepare for negotiations. Even if the offer is made at the asking price, you can always come up with a counteroffer, if there are multiple offers available. You have three options when you receive an offer from the buyer - you can accept the conditions, you can accept it after making some changes, or you can reject the offer.

Counteroffers are very common. It's like a tennis match between you and your potential buyers. Every ball that returns to your field tells you something. If the price does not change or changes slowly, you must either accept or decline it. After one or two messages back and forth with a slight price adjustment, the buyer will not move. At this point, you must accept or decline the offer.

Do not forget to find out the motives of the buyer for the purchase of your property. If you understand this, you can negotiate conditions other than the price. You can shorten the time for inspections and closures. They may also try to get them to pay taxes on the transfer of ownership fees, which may normally be the case for the seller. Ask them to cover a certain number of repairs that may occur after an inspection. There are many ways to improve an offer for you without changing the price.

Keep your emotions under control during negotiations, and do not take anything personally. After signing the contract, you may need to use the service before you graduate, and you do not want to deal with an angry buyer because you used to be uncomfortable.

If you have multiple offers on the table, you can use this to your advantage by playing them against each other. Returning to each potential buyer and telling them that you're getting better and better deals means you can increase the offer price and reduce or eliminate any unforeseen costs. Set the date and time when you will receive the best offers. If someone is interested in the property, they will respond in time.

When entering all bids, take into account all unforeseen expenses that can affect the bids you receive. For instance, you might have to close the sale of a property to pay for any financial exigency. If you have a bid for a low price and there are no worrying circumstances, then you can hold onto the property for a while longer. You don't always have to close the sale immediately. Remember that you are still in the negotiation phase and you have no reason to hurry, especially when all the external factors are favorable.

Also, you must ensure that you and the buyer agree to all the terms of sale and agree to it in writing. You need to have a watertight sale agreement including all the conditions both the parties agree to. Once this document is ready and everything is in order, it is time to seal the deal by signing the documents.

Sign the documents to transfer the file. Make sure that there are no errors. What are you doing when you have? Do you need a lawyer? What is the title company doing at their end?

Put simply, the deal is done when the buyer gives the seller money against a title deed. The buyer and the seller must be present at the closing together with their real estate agents, the closing agent and their lawyers, or any other practice that is common in your region.

If a lawyer does not visit you, make sure you receive all your final documents in advance. If you have no prior experience related to dealing with such transactions, then ensure that you have a lawyer present. Get the lawyer to draft the agreement and carefully go through it along with any fine print included in it before you sign it.

When this process of closing the deal comes to an end and both parties have signed the documents, make sure that the amount on the check you have left matches the amount on the payment form. If not, do not sign it until the amounts match. The withdrawal form is a record of legal transactions and must be correct.

The title agency you work with has already reviewed the history of property rights and hopefully will eliminate any existing ownership issues. You are the party that plans the closure. The title agent ensures that all numbers match, collects the appropriate signatures, authenticates, and issues checks. The title company is also responsible for registering the real estate law with the local government and the buyer's mortgage at the bank.

Chapter 36: Ongoing Mindset

You might have successfully flipped the property and done everything else to ensure that you can successfully sell the property for a profit. However, for some reason or another, you were unable to accomplish this goal. As an investor, you must be prepared for all possible scenarios. If you are unable to sell the flipped property, here are certain tips you can use to ensure that you can keep going.

As a real estate investor, if you experience positive feelings like joy, optimism, happiness, and even love, you will open yourself up to be more profitable and can benefit from investing in real estate. If you have set yourself a goal of making $1,000 per week, you will need to work towards achieving it. Once you get started, you will come across different investors with a positive mindset who have set higher goals for themselves. This will provide you with the necessary motivation and confidence to keep going. Surround yourself with people who are positive and who have got higher goals in life. Their enthusiasm and optimism are bound to rub off on you. If they can do it, so can you. You will learn that patience is a great virtue, and by being patient, you will be able to reap better profits. Don't be impatient and don't rush into something if you haven't thought it through. You needn't always make a big profit, and quite frankly that's not possible at all times. It is okay to make small profits as well. This will keep you going. Hang around with positive people, and this energy will rub off on you.

Positive thinking is quite a powerful tool. If you think positive thoughts, the outcome would be positive as well. Trust your gut, and keep a positive mindset. If you firmly believe that your investment will do well, it will prove that the market conditions are favorable. Don't be too scared to take a calculated risk. Weigh in the pros and cons before investing in something. It is bound to pay off. All successful investors have a good attitude toward investing. Your thoughts are powerful; there is no point in investing in something if you are always worried sick that it won't yield a good outcome.

You don't necessarily have to follow what others say or do. A successful investor often ignores what others have to say and would do the opposite of what is perceived to be the norm. In real estate investing, it is okay to ignore conventional wisdom. You needn't necessarily have to always invest in properties that are in nice parts of town. You can also invest in distressed homes if you see that they have got potential in them. If you want to, you can purchase properties at 20-30% under the market value, and you can purchase them for cash as well. You needn't always invest with the thought of appreciation in your mind. Instead, you should be able to recognize the potential in a property, then buy it even if others fail to see this potential.

It is all about having a positive mindset, and if you have this, you will make a handsome profit, it not immediately, then eventually.

Chapter 37: Mistake of the 99%

There are certain common mistakes that a lot of new investors make and these mistakes stand between you and the success you want. Here are a couple of common mistakes you must avoid making if you want to become a successful investor.

The Budget

Stick to the proposed budget. A common rookie mistake is not having sufficient funds to flip a property. Before you can flip or even purchase a property, you must ensure that you have the necessary financing available to complete the project you will be undertaking. You must always keep your finances in order and also leave some buffer funds for any unforeseen expenses. The ROI you can expect from the project depends on how well you have managed to budget and plan the project.

Business Plan

You need a good business plan before you get started with flipping houses. Make a list of all the short- and long-term goals you have set for yourself. Not only the goals, but you must also have a plan of action to attain those goals. Time is money, and this is especially true when investing in real estate. Having a good business plan will help set benchmarks to measure performance along with deadlines to complete the project. Apart from these things, it will also include the risks, opportunities, and the profitability quotient of the project.

Property Insurance

Buying property insurance before starting an investment project is a mistake for newcomers. Property insurance compensates homeowners and reduces the risk of dismantling projects if their property suffers damage such as theft, flood, or fire. If turning around is just a matter of repaying the original investment, you should do everything to protect your investment in the project. Investors can take out property insurance on the spot or over the Internet, but it is advisable to research thoroughly before making purchases as the premiums may vary.

Business Partners

Investors tend to seek help wherever they can find it, as a coup in the house is a tremendous effort. Do you have a buddy who says he's game if you can invest or fix? Think twice. Flipping a property can be stressful. Therefore, it is a good idea to work with those who are familiar with the process of flipping and know about all the work that's involved therein. If you decide to buddy up with your personal contacts, then ensure that the business relationship doesn't hamper your personal relationship.

Contractor

It is always a good idea to hire a reputable contractor and subcontractors to work on the flipping project. They must not only be adept at their work, but must also provide value for money. The costs incurred to hire such team members directly influences your ROI. If the property you are flipping happens to be a unique property, like a historic property, then it is best to work with someone who has experience handling these types of properties. A developer used to working with modern homes might not have the necessary skill and knowledge to work on restorative work for historic properties. Consult your real estate agent and other investors before you hire a contractor.

Lack of Knowledge

Just as the ignorance of your business partners puts you in a difficult position, an incomplete understanding of your market can also affect your investment performance. By conducting a market analysis, you can understand the risks and benefits of the areas you are reviewing and ensure that you successfully sell your home in reverse. You can also see if the best time to repair and refurbish a house in your area has arrived, and what the current trends in the housing market are. Market analysis and a business plan go hand in hand as both help investors to prepare for the duration of the home-acquisition process and what happens afterwards.

Exit Strategy

To make sure that you are successful in your business, you should always work out an "exit strategy" that largely depends on the price at which you listed the house. Contact your broker to determine the price listed, so you can quickly find the price of your home to reduce the time it costs to pay.

Good things take time, and flipping a property does not happen overnight. These are investments that require training, research, funding, skills, and a solid team. Take the right action and avoid these common mistakes to make your first home flip worthwhile.

Chapter 38: Final Checklist

Now that we have come to the end of this book, here is a final checklist you can refer to for ensuring that all the resources you need to flip a property successfully are at your fingertips whenever you need them:

- Learn the basics of real estate investing.

- Your reasons for choosing flipping properties to invest in real estate.

- The financial goals you wish to accomplish by flipping properties.

- Change your mindset and perspective about money.

- Overcome any misconceptions about getting rich quick and passive income.

- Stay motivated even when things don't seem to be going your way.

- Create a success mindset.

- Understand the different aspects of flipping a property.

- Evaluate all the risks involved.

- Set SMART goals for your investment venture.

- Study the trends in the real estate industry for 2019.

- Understand and learn to spot any manipulative tactics being used.

- Become a serious investor.

- Hire your dream team for flipping a property.
- Estimate the time required to complete flipping a property successfully.
- Search for properties you can flip and make a list of them.
- Analyze the properties.
- Choose the ideal property type for investment.
- Don't ignore foreclosures.
- Analyze all the different external factors that can influence your investment.
- Carefully go through all the regulations and do the due diligence essential for flipping a property.
- Make a checklist for viewing and buying a property.
- Calculate all the necessary financial ratios.
- Obtain the capital you need.
- Close the deal.
- Start to increase the value of the property.
- Make a list of all the repairs and renovation work you must undertake.
- Decide whether you can do it yourself or hire contractors.
- Make a list of the quick fixes you need to make.
- Negotiate with contractors to get the best possible

deals.

- Rehab and revamp the property.
- Sell the property.
- Close the sales deal.
- Have a backup plan for when things go south.
- Avoid the common mistakes other investors make.
- Keep a positive attitude and an ongoing mindset.

Once you can tick off all the things mentioned in this section, you are ready to get started with successfully flipping your first property.

Chapter 39: Keeping the Property for Rent

You can increase your assets and equity by investing in rental properties. This is a great way to make money. Now you need to calculate your margin so you can determine if real estate is the right investment decision or not. How do you calculate your fields? How much rent should you ask for? Making money is a numbers game, and you need to understand those numbers correctly.

When calculating the expected real estate return, consider the various costs that you incur in ownership of the property. Think about how these costs affect your bottom line. The profit margin is an important factor, and you should never skip this step. For example, if you decide to invest in stocks, you expect a return of between 5% and 8% per annum. What is the desired return? Do you expect an annual increase in this indicator, or are you satisfied with the constant return?

Think about the possible costs when buying a rental property. You can pay for it in two ways. You can take out a mortgage or pay in cash. For an investor just starting, this may seem a bit tense, but you have to take that into account. If you pay the property in cash, what are the possible opportunity costs? Much of your capital will be in the form of cash that you can't use for anything else. If you buy a house for $100,000 in cash, you expect at least an annual income of 6%. This means that you expect a monthly return of approximately $500. Regardless of your funding method, you need to be sure that the property you are investing in brings the income you are looking for.

If you are unable to sell the property after flipping it, then you can choose to rent out the property. By renting the property, the rent you earn from it can count as a steady cash flow for a specific period. If it looks like the market isn't favorable to make a sale for the next year, then instead of leaving the property vacant, it is a good idea to rent it out. Now, instead of a seller, you must think like a potential landlord. Here are some tips you can follow to get started.

Think Like the Tenant

A successful landlord will have to think like a tenant and take into consideration what's essential for them too. Tenants are your customers, so your ability to attract and retain them will depend upon your appreciation of their values, and thinking like a tenant will help you in picking the most suitable rental property.

Analyze the Property

You will need to identify the strengths and weaknesses of your property. Identify what your property has to offer and why it's different from that of your competitors. Once you have managed to start thinking like a tenant, it will be easier for you to be objective while determining the property's strengths and weaknesses. For instance, if you are renting out a two-bedroom condo that would be ideal for families, then it is important that you highlight that fact in your advertising copy as well. Perhaps you should emphasize that there's sufficient storage, that the building has additional facilities like a swimming pool, a gym, or reference its proximity to schools. Make sure that you aren't making up any details. Being aware of your property's weaknesses will help you in being realistic when you are positioning your property. If you know that there's another rental property on the market that offers better prospects than yours, then it doesn't make any sense to price your property at the same price or even higher.

Competition

If you are renting a two-bedroom condo, then you should collect information about every other two-bedroom condo that's available in the neighborhood. Remember to compare two similar things; it doesn't make any sense if you compare a modern two-bedroom to a condo that's twice its size. Once you have gathered all the information, then you will need to start thinking like a tenant again and evaluate your property for assessing its strengths and weaknesses and also those of the other, similar properties on the market. Does your competition happen to have more square footage, or is it situated in a better location? What is its layout? What are the additional facilities that they are offering? These are a few questions that you will have to ask yourself when you are evaluating your property.

Ideal Rent

Once you have understood your competition and also realized how well your property fares in comparison to theirs, then you will be able to figure out a rough estimate of expected rent. For instance, if the properties that offer better facilities than yours are priced at $1,200 a month, and those properties that provide fewer amenities are priced at $1,000 a month, you can expect rent that falls somewhere between these two.

Use the Data

Many investors tend to misuse historical data. It's an inaccurate misconception that just because a similar property rented for a specific price a year ago, it can be rented out for the same price even today. The market doesn't work like that. The past rental history of the unit is irrelevant because it needs to be evaluated, taking into consideration the needs of the present tenant. However, the past will give you some information to gauge whether or not you are on the right track. When it comes to pricing, it would be prudent to look at similar rentable properties that have been rented out for the last two months. For instance, a tentative price of $1,600 a month seems reasonable when similar properties have been rented out for $1,500 to $1,700 a month. However, if you try renting it out for $2,000, then it would trigger a red flag.

Adjust the Rent

You must adjust the pricing according to the demand in the market. When you are competing in the market for tenants, then you will need to evaluate just how intense your competition is, and this will help you in tweaking your pricing strategy. If you are competing against other two-bedroom condos in your neighborhood, then it does make sense to know how many of these condos are renting out every month and what they are going for in terms of rent. Your strategy might vary according to these answers. Your pricing policy should be fairly aggressive if you want to attract any tenants.

The rental market is always dynamic, and things keep changing. That's why you should revisit all the earlier stages for making sure that your pricing policy is competitive. Go through these steps every two weeks to make sure that you are strategically positioned in the rental market. Pricing your rental property in the right way takes more than just a lucky guess. It is a skill, and if you want to be successful, then you need to be a reasonable investor. It does take some time to figure it all out, but once you do, the time and effort spent on it will be well worth it.

Conclusion

I want to thank you once again for choosing this book. I hope it proved to be an enjoyable and informative read.

By now, you have come to understand the nuances of flipping properties and the reasons why others have become successful at flipping properties. Flipping houses is a great way to invest in real estate and can be a lucrative endeavor. However, there are certain things you must understand to become a successful investor. The different tips, steps, and information offered in this book will guide you through your journey of getting started with flipping houses and completing your first project.

Please understand that you need to be patient, consistent, and resilient in your efforts. There will be ups and downs. However, remember that it is all a learning experience and you will be able to attain your goals if you just keep going. Motivate yourself, learn about the real estate market, hire a good flipping team, and get started with flipping properties.

Now, all that's left for you to do is get out there as soon as you can and turn your financial goals into your future reality.

Thank you, and all the best for your future flipping endeavors!

References

Harris, J. (2019). 5 Reasons Why Real Estate Is a Great Investment. Retrieved from https://www.entrepreneur.com/article/304860

The Gotchas That'll Get Ya in House Flipping. (2019). Retrieved from https://connectedinvestors.com/blog/house-flipping-due-diligence-checklist/

Real Estate|Vault.com. (2019). Retrieved from https://www.vault.com/industries-professions/industries/real-estate

Myrick, C. (2019). Top 6 real estate scams – and how to avoid them. Retrieved from https://www.theglobeandmail.com/real-estate/mortgages-and-rates/top-6-real-estate-scams-and-how-to-avoid-them/article13108985/

Findlay-Shirras, G. (2019). Mastering An Abundance Mindset For Success In Real Estate - Become a local leader. Retrieved from https://www.becomealocalleader.com/inbound/mastering-an-abundance-mindset-for-success-in-real-estate/

Making passive income from real estate investment: 4 myths debunked - Easy Real Estate Money. (2019). Retrieved from https://www.easyrealestatemoney.com/2018/03/27/making-passive-income-real-estate-investment-4-myths-debunked/

M, A. (2019). 4 myths about flipping a house. Retrieved from https://www.saleezy.com.au/blog/article/4-myths-about-flipping-a-house.html

2019 Real Estate Trends: What You Need to Know. (2019).

Retrieved from https://www.daveramsey.com/blog/real-estate-trends

4 Types Of Home Renovation: Which Ones Boost Value?. (2019). Retrieved from https://www.investopedia.com/investing/types-home-renovation-which-ones-boost-value/

Do It Yourself (DIY) or Hire a Contractor for Home Improvement Projects?. (2019). Retrieved from https://www.moneycrashers.com/do-it-yourself-diy-hire-contractor-home-improvement/

Realistically, How Long Does it Take to Flip a House?. (2018). Retrieved from https://www.shermanbridge.com/blog/turnaround-time-flipping-properties/

Flipping Houses for Beginners: 6 Mistakes to Avoid | LendingHome Blog. (2018). Retrieved from https://www.lendinghome.com/blog/flipping-houses-for-beginners-6-mistakes-to-avoid/

10 Reasons to Invest in Real Estate | Strategic Investment Realtors. (2019). Retrieved from https://www.strategicinvestmentrealtors.com/reasons-invest-real-estate

LaCava, M. (2019). Flip Houses Fast Using These 11 Cheap Tips. Retrieved from https://www.biggerpockets.com/blog/2013/01/20/flip-houses-fast/

Eneriz, A. (2019). 13 Smart Ways to Sell Your Home as Fast as Possible. Retrieved from https://www.rd.com/home/improvement/sell-your-home-fast-as-possible/

Executive Sellers Realty. (2019). Retrieved from http://www.executivesellers.com/blog/top-6-real-estate-secrets/

Greene, D. (2018). The Top Seven Traits Of A Successful Real Estate Investor. Retrieved from https://www.forbes.com/sites/davidgreene/2018/11/18/the-top-seven-traits-of-a-a-successful-real-estate-investor/#371ba669378a

How to find Houses to Flip | Flipping Houses 101. (2019). Retrieved from https://rehabfinancial.com/flipping-houses-101/chapter-2-how-to-find-houses-to-flip/find-the-property-for-your-house-flip

Sbeih, A. (2019). Six Reasons Your Next Fix-and-Flip Should Be a Multi-Unit Dwelling | Socotra Capital - Hard Money Loans and Real Estate Lending. Retrieved from https://socotracapital.com/six-reasons-next-fix-flip-multi-unit-dwelling/

Koulopoulos, T. (2019). How to Negotiate Using the FBI's 5-Step Hostage Strategy. Retrieved from https://www.inc.com/thomas-koulopoulos/how-to-negotiate-using-the-fbis-5-step-hostage-strategy.html

Blankenship, R. (2018). Council Post: The Top 10 Risk Factors In Flipping Houses (And What To Do About Them). Retrieved from https://www.forbes.com/sites/forbesrealestatecouncil/2018/02/20/the-top-10-risk-factors-in-flipping-houses-and-what-to-do-about-them/#2bda14a23509

Money is NOT the root of all evil. (2019). Retrieved from https://www.nation.co.ke/lifestyle/women/Money-is-NOT-the-root-of-all-evil/1950830-2522436-bbs6wb/index.html

Goodwin, L. (2019). 20 Reasons Why a 9 to 5 Job Sucks. Retrieved from https://lanegoodwin.com/20-reasons-9-5-job-sucks/

Porter's Five Forces: - Understanding Competitive Forces to Maximize Profitability. (2019). Retrieved from https://www.mindtools.com/pages/article/newTMC_08.htm

Pasha, A. (2019). 5 Simple Ways To Stay Motivated As A Real Estate Entrepreneur. Retrieved from https://cashflowdiary.com/blog/real-estate/investing/5-simple-ways-to-stay-motivated-as-a-real-estate-entrepreneur/

10 Warning Signs To Look For Before Buying A House. (2019). Retrieved from https://www.financialsamurai.com/warning-signs-to-look-out-for-before-buying-a-house/

Eberlin, E. (2019). The Pros and Cons of Flipping a Property. Retrieved from https://www.thebalancesmb.com/pros-and-cons-of-flipping-a-property-2124830

How much does it REALLY cost to flip a house? | LendingHome Blog. (2019). Retrieved from https://www.lendinghome.com/blog/how-much-does-it-really-cost-to-flip-a-house/

Lieb, A. (2019). HuffPost is now a part of Oath. Retrieved from https://www.huffpost.com/entry/10-tips-for-strategically-negotiating-real-estate-deals_b_5952662ce4b0326c0a8d0b58

Williams, J. (2019). 4 Steps for Evaluating House Flipping Deals to Ensure Killer Profit. Retrieved from http://houseflippinghq.com/4-steps-evaluating-house-flipping-deals-ensure-killer-profit/

Building Relationships for a Successful Fix-and-Flip Business.

(2019). Retrieved from https://www.anchorloans.com/fix-and-flip/building-relationships-for-a-successful-fix-and-flip-business

Flipping Foreclosures | Know The Essentials To Making A Profit | House Flipping School. (2019). Retrieved from https://houseflippingschool.com/flipping-foreclosures-know-the-essentials/

www.ingramcontent.com/pod-product-compliance
Lightning Source LLC
Chambersburg PA
CBHW021820170526
45157CB00007B/2662